MW01232679

CODING

AND
PROGRAMMING
FOR BEGINNERS

A BEGINNERS GUIDE TO MICROSOFT ACCESS
AND C++ PROGRAMMING FAST AND EASY TO
LEARN

By Robert Coding

MS access

C++

MICROSOFT ACCESS

A BEGINNERS GUIDE TO MICROSOFT ACCESS STEP-BY-STEP

BY Robert Coding

Introduction

Microsoft Access is a database software that is used to save records for reporting, referencing and analysis MS access stores data in specific format, database specific to Access based Access Jet Database. With Microsoft Access, you can analyze big amount of data faster and more efficiently than with Excel or different forms of spreadsheets.

If you've been considering a database software to your enterprise, otherwise you're locating that traditional spreadsheets just aren't slicing it anymore, Microsoft Access simply what you're seeking out. Let's have a brief look of fundamental functions of access and how its functions can help the businesses to be more productive.

Access is maximum popular for its tables, forms and queries. The database tables are similar to spreadsheets, so that you shouldn't have an awful lot hassle the usage of the simple features of the program. But, it does take time to examine and master the full features. Tables have two things rows and columns. Rows represents set of related data and each row has the same structure in the whole table and every column in the table has the data value of particular type they both bifurcate categories, groups and more. Whilst putting in place a database, you may list the difficulty count of every column, just as you'll with a spreadsheet, and add as many columns as you'd like. While this is completed, every row leaves room for more statistics enter. One characteristic that users surely like is they don't want to finalize the tables manually. Additionally, get right of entry to has a query feature that permits facts to be mixed from more than one desk, and you could even specify the conditions. This saves numerous time due to the fact you don't ought to glance through rows and rows of statistics.

If you're already the usage of a spreadsheet application like Excel, you're acquainted with the benefits of organizing your facts. However, allows appearance further into some of the particular obligations that you can perform with Access.

- Preserve all records for each patron or purchaser, which include addresses, invoices, payment and order statistics.
- Keep track of economic statistics without having a separate software program application. If you have the overall Microsoft workplace Suite, you may even set fee reminders.
- Manage advertising and income thanks to having all customer facts within the database. Ship out flyers, emails and coupons and song how customers respond.
- Track manufacturing and inventory with the aid of getting into statistics on shipments and additionally knowing whilst it's time to order more of a specific product.

Run reviews and analyses using the reports and charts. You can basically run a document on something within a rely of mins, such as customers who are behind on price.

Access follows most, however not all, conventional database terminology. The terms database, table, file, field, and value imply a hierarchy from largest to smallest. These identical terms are used with simply all database structures. Generally, the phrase database is a computer term for a set of statistics concerning a sure subject matter or business software. Databases assist you prepare this associated records in a logical style for clean get entry to and retrieval. Databases aren't only for computer systems. There are also manual databases; we once in a while discuss with those as guide filing structures or manual database systems. These submitting systems usually consist of people, papers, folders, and submitting shelves paper is the important thing to a manual records base machine. In manual database systems, you commonly have inside and outside baskets and some sort of formal filing method. You get entry to statistics manually by means of opening a report cabinet, taking away a document folder, and locating the proper piece of paper. Users fill out paper forms for input, perhaps via using a keyboard to input records that's printed on forms. You discover information via manually sorting the papers or by way of copying statistics from many papers to some other piece of paper (or even into an Excel spreadsheet). You can use a spreadsheet or calculator to investigate the data or show it in new and thrilling approaches. An get entry to database is not anything greater than an automated model of the filing and retrieval capabilities of a paper submitting gadget. Get right of entry to databases store facts in a carefully defined shape. Access tables store a diffusion of various sorts of information, from easy lines of text (which includes call and cope with) to complex statistics (together with photographs, sounds, or video snap shots). Storing records in a unique layout allows a database management gadget (DBMS) like access to show statistics into beneficial statistics. Tables function the number one statistics repository in an get admission to database. Queries, bureaucracy, and reports offer get right of entry to the records, enabling a person to feature or extract records and supplying the statistics in beneficial methods. Most developers upload macros or visible primary for programs (VBA) code to paperwork and reviews to make their get right of entry to applications simpler to apply. A relational database control machine (RDBMS), such as get entry to, stores statistics in related tables. As an example, a table containing worker data (names and addresses) can be related to a desk containing payroll facts (pay date, pay amount, and check range). Queries allow the consumer to invite complicated questions From these related tables, with the answers displayed as onscreen forms and printed reports. One of the essential differences between a relational database and manual filing system device is that, in a relational database machine, data for single individual or item may be saved in separate tables. As an example, in affected person control system, the affected person's name, deal with, and other contact statistics is possibly to be stored in extraordinary table from the table protecting affected person treatments. In fact, the table holds all treatment information for all patients, and a patient identifier (typically more than a few) is used to appearance up an individual affected person's treatments in the treatment table. In Microsoft Access, a database is the general box for the data and related gadgets. It's greater than the gathering of tables, however a database consists of many sorts of objects, including queries, forms, reviews, macros, and code modules. As you open an MS Access database, the objects (tables, queries, indexes, procedures, triggers and so on) inside the database are provided that allows you to work with. You may open several copies MS Access to on the identical time and simultaneously work with a couple of database, if its needed.

Chapter 1

1.1 Database Development

Microsoft Access follows most, however now not all, conventional database terminology. The terms database, table, record, field, and value imply a hierarchy from largest to smallest. These identical terms are used with simply all database structures.

1.1.1 Tables

A table is only a box for raw information (known as data), just like a folder in a person manual submitting filing system. Every table in ma Microsoft Access database incorporates information approximately a single topic, which include employees or merchandise, and the statistics within the table is organized into rows and columns. In Access, a table is an entity. As you layout and build access databases, or even when running with an updated existing Microsoft software application, you must think of how the tables and different database items represent the physical entities controlled via your database and the way the entities relate to one another. When you create a table, you can view the table in a spreadsheet like shape, referred to as a datasheet, comprising rows and columns. Even though a datasheet and a spreadsheet are superficially similar, a datasheet is a completely one of a kind of item.

1.1.2 Records and fields

A datasheet is split into rows (known as records) and columns (called fields), with the first row (the heading on top of each column) containing the names of the fields in the database. Each row is a single document containing fields which might be associated with that document. In a manual gadget, the rows are individual forms (sheets of paper), and the fields are equivalent to the blank areas on a printed shape which you fill in.

Each column is a field that consists of many properties that explain the type of data contained within the field and how access need to handle the field's information. Those properties encompass the name of the (Agency) and the type of information inside the field (textual content). A field may additionally consist of different properties as well. As an instance, the location fields property tells to Access the maximum number of characters a location field can hold.

1.1.3 Values

At the intersection of a record and a field is a value the real information detail. As an example, if you have a field known as Agency, an employer name entered into that field might constitute one facts value. Positive guidelines govern how statistics is contained in an get entry to table.

1.2 Relational Database

Microsoft Access is a relational database management system. Access data is stored in related tables, wherein facts in one table (including clients) is related to facts in every other table (such as Orders). Access continues the relationships among associated tables, making it clean to extract a consumer and all of the client's orders, without losing any facts or pulling order records not owned via the Client. Multiple tables simplify data entry and reporting by way of lowering the enter of redundant data. Via defining two tables for a software that uses purchaser records, for instance, you don't need to store the clients call and deal with every time the purchaser purchases an item.

When you've created the tables, they need to be associated with each other. As an example, if You have a client's table and a sales table, you can relate the two tables the usage of a common discipline between them. In this case, customer number might be an amazing discipline to have in each tables. This will let you see income in the sales table where the client number suits the clients table.

The benefit of this model is which you don't ought to repeat key attributes about a client's (like patron call, cope with, metropolis, nation, zip) on every occasion you add a new file to the income desk. All you need is the client number. Whilst a client changes address, for instance, the deal with modifications simplest in one record within the clients table.

Keeping apart information into more than one tables within a database makes a system less complicated to hold due to the fact all statistics of a given type are in the equal table. By using taking the time to properly segment data into a couple of tables, you revel in an enormous reduction in design and work time. This procedure is known as normalization.

Chapter 2

2.1 Microsoft Database Objects

In case you're new to databases (or maybe in case you're an experienced database user), you need to understand some key concepts earlier than starting to construct Microsoft Access databases. The access records-base consists of six sorts of pinnacle-degree items, which encompass the facts and gear which you want to use access:

- Table: Holds the actual records
- Query: Searches for, sorts, and retrieves unique records
- Form: lets you input and display facts in a custom designed layout
- Report: shows and prints formatted data
- Macro: Automates obligations without programming
- Module: carries programming statements written within the VBA programming language

2.1.1 Tables

As you've located in advance on previous chapter, tables function the primary facts repository in an get admission to database. You have interaction with tables through a unique type of object known as a statistics- sheet. Even though not a permanent database object, a datasheet displays a table's content material in a row and column layout, just like an Excel worksheet. A datasheet displays a desk's records in a raw shape, without alterations or filtering. The Datasheet view is the default mode for displaying all fields for all records. You can scroll via the datasheet using the directional keys on your keyboard. You can also display associated facts in other tables even as in a datasheet. In addition, you could make modifications to the displayed statistics.

2.1.2 Queries

Queries extract facts from a database. A question selects and defines a collection of information that satisfy a sure circumstance. Most forms and reviews are primarily based on queries that integrate, filter, or type information earlier than it's displayed. Queries are often known as from macros or VBA procedures to trade, add, or delete database facts. An example of a query is while a person at the sales workplace tells the database, "show me all clients, in alphabetical order through name, who are placed in Massachusetts and acquired a few issue over the last six months" or "show me all customers who sold Chevrolet vehicle fashions within the past six months and show them looked after by using purchaser name after which by sale date." In place of asking the query in plain English, someone makes use of the question by means of instance (QBE) approach. While you enter commands into the query fashion designer window and run the question, the question interprets the commands into established query Language (SQL) and retrieves the favored information.

2.2 Information access and show forms

Data entry forms help customers get facts into a database table quick, easily, and accurately. Facts-access and show paperwork offer a greater based view of the records than what a datasheet offers. From this dependent view, database data may be considered, added, modified, or deleted. Entering information via the records-access paperwork is the maximum common manner to get the information into the database table. Facts access forms may be used to limit get admission to sure fields within the desk. Paperwork can also be better with records validation guidelines or VBA code to test the validity of your facts before it's delivered to the database table. Most users opt to enter records into facts-entry bureaucracy instead of into Datasheet perspectives of tables. Paperwork frequently resemble acquainted paper documents and can useful resource the person with statistics-entry responsibilities. Bureaucracy make records entry easy to recognize by means of guiding the consumer via the fields of the desk being up to date. Examine simplest forms are frequently used for inquiry purposes. These paperwork display positive fields inside a table. Showing some fields and not others way that you could restrict a consumer's get entry to touchy statistics while permitting get right of entry to different fields within the same table.

2.3 Reports

Reports provides you facts in PDF-fashion formatting. Get right of entry to permits for a super amount of pliability while creating reports. As an instance, you can configure a document to list all records in a given table (consisting of a client's table), or you may have the file include simplest the data assembly sure criteria (together with all clients residing in Arizona). You try this by way of basing the document on a query that selects handiest the facts wished via the file. Reviews frequently integrate more than one tables to provide complicated relationships among unique sets of records. An example is printing a bill. The clients table provides the customer's call and address (and different applicable records) and associated statistics within the sales table to print the man or woman line-object facts for every product ordered. The record also calculates the sales totals and prints them in a particular format. Moreover, you may have got entry to output records into an invoice file, a broadcast record that summarizes the invoice.

2.4 Macros and VBA

Just as Excel has macros and VBA programming functionality, Microsoft get admission to has its equivalents. That is where the genuine energy and versatility of Microsoft get admission to statistics analysis resides. Whether or not you're the use of them in custom capabilities, batch evaluation, or automation, macros and VBA modules can add a customized flexibility that is hard to fit the usage of every other method. As an instance, you could use macros and VBA to routinely perform redundant analyses and habitual analytical approaches, leaving you free to work on other tasks. Macros and VBA also can help you reduce the risk of human mistakes and to make certain that analyses are preformed the same way every time. Starting in bankruptcy 22, you will discover the advantages of macros and VBA, and learn how you could use them to schedule and run batch analysis.

2.5 Planning for database objects

To create database gadgets, which include tables, forms, and reviews, you first complete a sequence of layout obligations. The better your design is, the higher your utility could be. The extra you watched through your design, the quicker and greater correctly you may whole any system. The layout method isn't a few important evil, neither is its rationale to provide voluminous amounts of documentation. The sole intent of designing an object is to supply a clear path to comply with as you enforce it.

Chapter 3

3.1 Five Step Design Model

The 5 design steps defined in this segment offer a strong basis for developing database applications together with tables, queries, forms, reports, macros, and easy VBA modules.
The time you spend on each step depends absolutely on the situations of the database you're building. As an instance, occasionally customers provide you with an example of a file they need printed from Microsoft Access database, and the assets of information at the report are so obvious that designing the document takes a few minutes. Other instances, especially when the users' requirements are complicated or the enterprise strategies supported by the software require an exceptional deal of research, you could spend many days on Step 1.

Step 1: the general design—from concept to reality

All software developers face similar problems, the primary of that is figuring out a way to meet the desires of the end consumer. It's important to apprehend the general user requirements earlier than zeroing in on the details.

For example, your users can also ask for a database that supports the following obligations:

- Coming into and retaining clients information facts (name, address, and economic history)
- Entering and retaining income data (income date, payment approach, total quantity, patron identification, and other fields)
- Coming into and retaining sales line item records (information of objects bought)
- Viewing facts from all of the tables (income, clients, sales line objects, and bills)
- Asking all types of questions about the records in the database
- Generating a month-to-month invoice record
- Producing a consumer income history
- Generating mailing labels and mail-merge reviews

When reviewing these eight duties, you can need to remember different peripheral responsibilities that weren't referred to with the aid of the person. Earlier than you soar into designing, sit down and find out how the present process works. To perform this, you have to do a thorough wishes analysis of the existing gadget and how you would possibly automate it. Prepare a sequence of questions that deliver perception to the patron's commercial enterprise and the way the customer uses his facts. For instance, whilst considering automating any type of commercial enterprise, you might ask those questions:

- What reviews and paperwork are presently used?
- How are sales, customers, and other data presently stored?
- How are billings processed?

As you ask these questions and others, the patron will probably bear in mind different things about the commercial enterprise which you must understand. A walkthrough of the present procedure is likewise helpful to get a sense for the commercial enterprise. You may have to pass back numerous times to take a look at the present procedure and the way the personnel work. As you put together to finish the remaining steps, hold the patron worried permit the users know what you're doing and ask for enter on what to perform, ensuring it's in the scope of the person's needs.

Step 2: record design

Even though it can appear odd to start with reviews, in lots of instances, users are extra inquisitive about the printed output from a database than they're in every other aspect of the utility. Reports often consist of each bit of data managed via a utility. Due to the fact reports have a tendency to be complete, they're often the fine way to acquire vital statistics approximately a database's necessities. Whilst you see the reviews that you'll create on this section, you may surprise, "Which comes first, the bird or the egg?" Does the document layout come first, or do you first decide the statistics gadgets and text that make up the file? Without a doubt, those gadgets are considered at the equal time. It isn't critical the way you lay out the records in a document. The extra time you're taking now, how- ever, the less complicated it will likely be to assemble the file. A few people pass so far as to place grid- lines on the record to discover precisely where they want every little bit of records to be.

Step 3: statistics design

The subsequent step within the layout phase is to take a stock of all the facts needed through the reviews. One of the great techniques is to listing the information gadgets in each file. As you accomplish that, take cautious word of gadgets which might be protected in multiple report. Make certain which you preserve the identical name for a data item this is in more than one document because the facts object is truly the equal item.

As you can see by comparing the form of consumer records wanted for every document, there are many common fields. Maximum of the patron records fields are located in each reports. Table 1.1 indicates only some of the fields that are utilized in every report those related to customer information. Due to the fact the related row and field names are the identical, you could easily ensure which you have all the statistics objects. Although finding items without problems isn't critical. For this small database, it will become very important when you have to address large tables containing many fields.

Table # 3.1: Clients related data items found in reports

Clients Report	Invoice Report
Clients Name	Clients Name
Street	Street
City	City
State	State
Zip Code	Zip Code
Phone Number	Phone Numbers
Email Address	
Web Address	
Last Sales Date	
Sales Tax Rate	

As you could see when you observe the sort of income statistics wished for the file, some items (fields) are repeating (for example, the Product bought, quantity bought, and charge of object fields). Every bill could have more than one objects, and every of these objects desires the identical kind of records—number ordered and rate according to object. Many sales have multiple bought object. Also, every bill may additionally include partial payments, and it's viable that this charge information can have a couple of lines of charge statistics, so these repeating objects may be put into their own grouping.

Table # 3.2: Dales data found in reports

Invoice report	Item data
Invoice date	Product purchased
Sales date	Quantity purchased
Invoice date	Description of item
Payment method	Item price
Salesperson	Discount per item
Discounts	
Tax location	
Product purchased	
Quantity purchased	
Description of item	
Price of item	
Payment type	
Payment date	
Payment amount	
Expiration date	

You may take all the individual items which you discovered within the income records institution inside the preceding section and extract them to their very own institution for the bill report. Desk 1.2 indicates the statistics related to every line object. After extracting the client facts, you could flow on to the sales records. In this case, you need to research handiest the invoice document for information items which are precise to the sales. Table 1.2 lists the fields inside the record that include information approximately income.

Step 4: desk design

Now for the hard part: you ought to decide which fields are needed for the tables that make up the reports. While you examine the multitude of fields and calculations that make up the various files you have, you begin to see which fields belong to the various tables inside the database. (You already did tons of the preliminary paintings by means of arranging the fields into logical corporations.) For now, encompass each field you extracted. You'll want to add others later (for numerous motives), although positive fields won't appear in any table. It's essential to understand that you don't want to feature each little bit of data into the database's tables. As an instance, users may additionally need to feature excursion and different out of office days to the database to make it smooth to recognize which employees are available on a selected day. But, it's very smooth to burden an application's initial layout by means of incorporating too many ideas at some stage in the initial development levels. Because get entry to tables are so smooth to modify later, it's in all likelihood high quality to place aside noncritical items until the preliminary design is entire. Generally speaking, it's not difficult to deal with consumer requests after the database improvement project is underway.

When you've used each record to display all the records, it's time to consolidate the data through purpose (for instance, grouped into logical organizations) after which evaluate the facts throughout those functions. To do that step, first examine the client data and combine all its different fields to create a single set of information objects. Then do the identical component for the sales information and the line-object statistics.

Table # 3.3: Comparing data items

Clients data	Invoice data	Line items	Payment info
Client agency name	Invoice number	Product purchased	Payment
Street	Date of sale	Quantity purchased	Date of payment
City	Date of invoice	Description of purchasing	Amount of purchaser
State	Discount	Price of item	Credit card no.
Zip code	Tax rate	Each item discount	Date of expiry
Phone no.			
Email address			
Web address			
Discount rate			
Client since			
Sales tax			

Consolidating and comparing records is a superb manner to begin developing the character desk, but you've got a lot more to do. As you learn greater about the way to carry out a records design, you furthermore might study that the clients data ought to be break up into two organizations. Some of these gadgets are used best once for every customer, even as other items may additionally have more than one entries. An example is the income column the charge statistics could have multiple traces of statistics. You need to in addition ruin these forms of records into their own columns, accordingly, separating all associated types of items into their personal columns an instance of the normalization part of the design process. For example, one customer may have multiple contacts with the agency or make a couple of payments in the direction of a single sale. Of course, we've already damaged the records into 3 classes: patron statistics, invoice statistics, and line object information.

Remember the fact that one patron can also have a couple of invoices, and every bill might also have multiple line gadgets on it. The bill data class consists of data about man or woman income and the road-objects category incorporates data about each invoice. Word that those 3 columns are all related; as an example, one customer can have more than one invoices, and each invoice may also require multiple line items.

The relationships among tables can be different. For instance, each income bill has one and simplest one customer, whilst each purchaser can also have a couple of income. A comparable courting exists among the sales bill and the line items of the invoice.

Database table relationships require a unique field in each tables worried in a dating. A unique identifier in every table allows the database engine to properly join and extract associated facts. Best the income desk has a completely unique identifier (bill wide variety), which means that that you need to add at the least one field to every of the other tables to serve as the link to other tables for example, adding a client identification area to the clients desk, including the same subject to the invoice table, and establishing a relationship among the tables through purchaser id in each desk. The database engine makes use of the connection between customers and invoices to attach customers with their invoices.

Relationships among tables are facilitated through the usage of key fields.

Table # 1.4: table with keys

Clients data	Invoice data	Line items	Payment Data
Client ID	Invoice ID	Invoice ID	Invoice ID
Clients Name	Clients ID	Line No	Payment type
City	Date of invoice	Description of purchasing	Amount of purchaser
State	Discount	Price of item	Credit card no.
Zip code	Tax rate	Each item discount	Date of expiry
Phone no.			
Email address			
Web address			
Discount rate			
Client since			
Sales tax			

With an know how of the need for linking one fields to another table, you could upload the desired key fields to every group. Table 1.4 shows two new agencies and hyperlink fields created for each organization of fields. Those linking fields, known as primary keys and foreign keys, are used to hyperlink these tables together.

The sector that uniquely identifies each row in a desk is the number one key. The corresponding subject in a related desk is the foreign key. In our instance, customer identification inside the clients table is a number one key, even as customer identification within the Invoices desk is a foreign key. Let's count on a certain record within the clients table has 12 in its purchaser id discipline. Any document inside the Invoices desk with 12 as its purchaser identification is "owned" by client 12. With the key fields brought to each desk, you could now find a discipline in every table that hyperlinks

It to other tables within the database. For instance, desk 1.4 indicates patron identity in both the clients desk (where it's the number one key) and the invoice desk (in which it's a foreign key). You've diagnosed the 3 middle tables on your device, as reflected with the aid of the first three columns in table 1.4. That is the general, or first, cut in the direction of the very last desk designs. You've also created an additional truth desk to maintain the sales payment statistics. Commonly, charge details aren't part of an income bill. Taking time to properly layout your database and the tables contained within it is arguably the maximum essential step in developing a database orientated application. By using designing your database efficaciously, you preserve manage of the records, disposing of highly priced records entry mistakes and proscribing your records entry to essential fields.

Although this e book isn't geared toward coaching database principle and all its nuances, this is a great region to briefly describe the artwork of database normalization. You'll study the info of normalization in chapter four, however in the interim you must recognize that normalization is the method of breaking records down into constituent tables. Earlier on this chapter you read approximately how many access builders upload distinctive information, which includes customers, invoice statistics, and invoice line objects, into one big table. A massive table containing varied statistics quickly will become unwieldy and difficult to keep updated. Because a patron's telephone variety seems in every row containing that customer's facts, more than one updates need to be made when the phone variety modifications.

Step 5: form layout

Once you've created the data and set up table relationships, it's time to design your paperwork. Paperwork are made up of the fields that can be entered or considered in Edit mode. Generally speaking, your get entry to displays must appearance a lot like the paperwork utilized in a manual device.

Whilst you're designing bureaucracy, you need to area three types of objects onscreen:

- Labels and textual content box information access fields: The fields on get entry to forms and reports are called controls.
- Unique controls (command buttons, more than one-line text boxes, alternative buttons, list containers, take a look at packing containers, commercial enterprise graphs, and images).
- Graphical gadgets to decorate the forms (colorations, lines, rectangles, and 3 dimensional results).

Preferably, if the form is being evolved from a present revealed shape, the get right of entry to information-access form have to resemble the broadcast form. The fields ought to be in the identical relative area at the screen as they may be inside the published counterpart. Labels show messages, titles, or captions. Text boxes provide an area in which you may kind or show textual content or numbers that are contained in your database. Test boxes suggest a situation and are either unchecked or checked. Different kinds of controls available with access consist of command buttons, list packing containers, combo packing containers, choice buttons, toggle buttons, and choice agencies.

Chapter 4

4.1 Microsoft Access Tables

4.2 Table types

To Microsoft Access, a table is constantly just a table. But to your Microsoft Access application, specific tables serve special functions. A database table fits into one among 3 sorts: an item table, a transaction table, or a join desk. Knowing what form of table, you're developing facilitates to decide the way you create it.

4.2.1 Object tables

Object tables are the most not unusual. Each record of this type of desk holds facts that relates to real world object. A client is a real-world object, and a record in a table named tblclient holds information approximately of the client. The fields in an object table mirror the traits of the item they represents. A city field in the table describes one function of the client particularly, the actual city where the purchaser is. Whilst developing an object table, reflect on consideration on the traits of that item that make it precise or that are vital.

4.2.2 Transaction tables

The next most common type of table is a transaction table. Each file of a transaction table holds information about an event. Like you have placed the order for a book so placing an order for a book is an instance of an event. To hold the info of all the orders, you may have a table named tblbookorders. Transaction tables almost constantly have a date/time discipline due to the fact while the event happened is usually a crucial piece of records to file. Some other not unusual form of subject is an area that refers to an objects table, together with a connection with the purchaser in tblclient that placed the order. While growing a transaction table, consider the statistics created via the occasion and who changed into involved.

4.2.3 Join tables

Join tables are the easiest to design and are vitally critical to a highly designed database. Normally bearing on tables is a simple procedure: a client orders a book, for instance, and you could without problems relate that order to that client. However now and again the connection isn't so clear. A book might also have many authors, and an author may additionally have many books. Whilst this relationship exists, called a many-to-many relationship, a be a part of table sits in the center of the two tables. A be part of desk typically has a call that displays the association, including tblauthorbook. A be part of desk normally has only 3 fields: a completely unique subject to become aware of every file, a reference to 1 side of the association, and a connection with the other side of an affiliation.

4.3 Creating a new table

Developing database tables is as much art as it's far science. Obtaining a very good working know how of the clients necessities is a fundamental step for any new database assignment.

In this chapter, we will create primary access tables. In the following sections, you'll look at the procedure of adding tables to an access database, including the extraordinarily complicated challenge of choosing the right records kind to assign to every discipline in a table. It's constantly an excellent idea to plan tables first, earlier than you operate the get entry to equipment to add tables to the database. Many tables, in particular small ones, actually don't require a lot of forethought before adding them to the database. In any case, now not an awful lot making plans is needed to layout a desk protecting research facts, inclusive of the names of towns and states. But, more complex entities, including clients and products, commonly require substantial idea and attempt to implement well.

Despite the fact that you can layout the desk without any forethought as you create it in get entry to, care- completely planning a database machine is a superb concept. You could make changes later, but doing so wastes time; commonly, the result is a machine that's tougher to preserve than one that you've planned nicely from the beginning. Within the following sections, we discover the brand new, blank table introduced to the chapter04.msaccdb database. It's crucial to apprehend the steps required to add new tables to an access database.

Designing a table

1. Create a new table
2. Enter field names, properties, data types and descriptions if you want
3. Select and set the primary key for the table
4. Create indexes for the field necessary
5. Now save the tables design

Usually talking, a few tables are in no way definitely completed. As users' needs trade or the commercial enterprise rules governing the application exchange, you would possibly find it vital to open an existing desk in design view. This book, like maximum books on MS Access, describes the manner of creating tables as if each table you ever work on is modern. The truth is, however, that most of the work that you do on an Access is completed on current gadgets in the database. Some of the ones objects you've brought yourself, at the same time as different gadgets may additionally have been brought by every other developer at a while in the beyond. However, the technique of preserving a current database aspect could be very tons the same as growing the equal object from scratch. Begin by means of choosing the Create tab at the Ribbon on the top of the Access display screen. The Create tab (proven in discern 4.1) carries all the equipment important to create not handiest tables, but also forms, reports, and other database objects.

Figure # 4.1

The Create tab contains tools necessary for adding new objects to your Access database.

There are two main methods to add new tables to an get entry to database, each of which are invoked from the Tables group at the Create tab:

- Clicking the table button provides a table in Datasheet view to the database with one autonumber field named identity
- Clicking the table design button adds a table in design view to the database

For this case, we'll be the use of the table design button, but first, permit's take a look at the
Table button.

Clicking the table button provides a new table to the MS Access environment. The new table appears in Datasheet view inside the location to the right of the Navigation pane. The new table is proven in determine 4.2. Be aware that the new table seems in Datasheet view, with an identity column already inserted and a click to add column to the proper of the id field.

Figure # 4.2

The new table in Datasheet view.

The click to add column is supposed to allow clients to fast upload fields to a table. All you need to do is start entering facts within the new column. You assign the field a name by means of right clicking the field's heading, selecting Rename subject, and coming into a name for the field. In different words, constructing an get admission to table can be very much like growing a spreadsheet in Excel. After you've added the new column, the gear on the Fields tab of the Ribbon (shown in discern 4.3) allow you to set the precise facts kind for the sphere, alongside its formatting, validation regulations, and other houses.

Figure # 4.3

Field design tools are located on the Fields tab of the Ribbon.

The second one technique of adding new tables is to click on the desk design button inside the Tables group at the Create tab. Get entry to opens a new table in design view, permitting you to feature fields to the desk's layout. Figure 4.4 indicates a new table's layout after a few fields were introduced. Table layout view affords a quite greater deliberate technique to building access tables.

Figure # 4.4

A new table added in Design view.

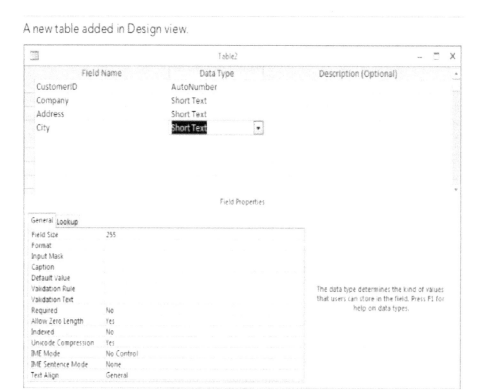

The table design is simple to apprehend, and every column is clearly labeled. On some distance left is the field name column, where you input the names of fields you add to the table. You assign a data type to every field in the table and (optionally) offer a description for the field. Statistics types are mentioned in detail later in this chapter.

For this exercising, you create the clients table for the Collectible Mini cars application. The fundamental layout of this table is printed in table 3.1. We cover the information of this table's design within the "creating tblclients" section, later in this chapter.

Table # 4.1: Mini Car Client's Table

Field name	Data type	Description
Clients ID	Auto number	Primary key
Agency	Short text	Employer contact
Address	Short text	Contact address
City	Short text	Contact city
State	Short text	Contact state
Zip code	Short text	Contact zip code
Phone	Short text	Contact phone
Fax	Short text	Contact fax
Email	Short text	Contact email
Website	Short text	Contact web address
Credit limit	Currency	Credit limit of customers in dollar
Current balance	Currency	Current balance of customers in dollars
Credit status	Short text	Description of customers credit status
Active	Y/N	Whether client is still buying or selling to mini cars

4.4 Design tab

Figure # 4.5

The Design tab of the Ribbon.

4.4.1 Primary key

Click on this button to designate which of the fields within the table you need to use because the tables primary key. Traditionally, the primary key seems on the top of the list of fields inside the table, but it may appear anywhere in the table's layout.

4.4.2 Insert row

Although it makes little difference to the database engine, many builders are fussy approximately the sequence of fields in a table. Many of the wizards in get entry to show the fields inside the identical order because the table. Keeping a address field over the city field can make developments much easier. Clicking the Insert Rows button inserts a blank row just above the position occupied by way of the mouse cursor. As an example, if the cursor is presently within the 2nd row of the table designer, clicking the Insert Rows button inserts an empty row within the 2nd role, shifting the present 2nd row to the 3rd position

4.4.3 Delete row

Clicking the Delete Rows button gets rid of a row from the table's design.

4.4.4 Property Sheet

Clicking the property Sheet button opens the property Sheet for the complete table (proven in figure 4.6). Those properties permit you to specify essential table traits, together with a validation rule to apply to the entire table, or an exchange sort order for the desk's information.

Figure # 4.6

The Property Sheet.

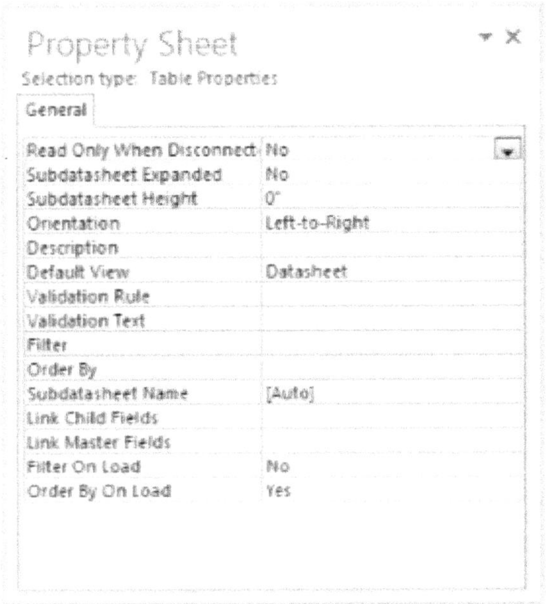

Property Sheet	▾ ✕
Selection type: Table Properties	
General	
Read Only When Disconnect	No ▾
Subdatasheet Expanded	No
Subdatasheet Height	0"
Orientation	Left-to-Right
Description	
Default View	Datasheet
Validation Rule	
Validation Text	
Filter	
Order By	
Subdatasheet Name	[Auto]
Link Child Fields	
Link Master Fields	
Filter On Load	No
Order By On Load	Yes

4.4.5 Indexes

Indexes are discussed in a great deal more element within the "Indexing access Tables" phase, later on this bankruptcy. Clicking the Indexes button opens the Indexes conversation box, which permits you to specify the information of indexes at the fields in your table.

4.5 Working with fields

You create fields with the aid of coming into an area call and a subject information kind in the top area entry vicinity of the table layout window. The (optionally available) Description property may be used to signify the sphere's purpose. The outline appears within the popularity bar at the bottom of the display for the duration of records access and may be beneficial to humans working with the utility. After coming into every subject's call and records kind, you can in addition specify how every area is utilized by getting into properties within the field properties area.

4.6 Naming a discipline

An area call should be descriptive enough to become aware of the field to you because the developer, to the consumer of the system, and to MS Access. Field names ought to be long enough to quick identify the purpose of the field, however now not overly lengthy. (Later, as you enter validation guidelines or use the field name in a calculation, you'll need to save yourself from typing lengthy field names.)

To enter a subject name, role the pointer within the first row of the table design window beneath the sphere call column. Then type a valid field name, watching these guidelines:

- Field names may be from 1 to 64 characters in its length.
- Field name can include letters, numbers, and special characters, besides period (.),
Exclamation mark (!), accent grave (`), and brackets ([]).
- Field names can consist of spaces. Spaces ought to be avoided in field names for some of
The same motives you keep away from them in table names.
- You couldn't use low order ASCII character as an example Ctrl+J or Ctrl+L (ASCII values
0 to 31).
- You mayn't begin with a blank space.

You can enter field names in uppercase, lowercase, or mixed case. In case you make a mistake even as typing the field name, function the cursor wherein you want to make a correction and kind the alternate. You can exchange a field name at any time, even if the table includes data.

Chapter 5

5.1 data types

When you enter a field, you must also decide what kind of records every of your fields will hold. In MS Access, you can pick any of several data types.

Short text

The short text data type holds facts that is virtually and simply characters (letters, numbers, punctuation). Names, addresses, and descriptions are all text data, as are numeric facts that aren't utilized in a calculation (inclusive of telephone numbers, Social safety numbers, and zip codes). Although you specify the scale of each quick textual content field within the property region, you could input no extra than 255 characters of information in any quick textual content area. Get right of entry to makes use of variable length fields to shop textual content records. If you designate a discipline to be 25 characters huge and you use simplest five characters for every report, then handiest enough room to save 5 characters is used on your database.
You'll find that the ACCDB database report would possibly fast grow quite huge, but textual content fields are commonly no longer the cause. However, it's correct practice to restriction quick textual content subject widths to the maximum you believe is likely for the sphere. Names can be complicated due to the fact pretty long names are not unusual in some cultures. But, it's a safe guess that a postal code can be fewer than 12 characters, while a U.S. state abbreviation is usually 2 characters. By limiting a short textual content field's width, you furthermore may limit the number of characters customers can input whilst the sphere is utilized in a form.

Long text

The long text data type holds a variable quantity of statistics up to 1GB. Long text data types use handiest as a lot memory as important for the data stored. So, if one record uses one hundred characters, some other requires only 10, and yet another wishes 3,000, you use only as plenty area as each report calls for. You don't specify a field length for the long text data type. Access allocates as a whole lot area as essential for the data.

Number

The wide variety of data type allows you to enter numeric information that is, numbers so one can be utilized in mathematical calculations or represent scalar portions consisting of stock counts. (when you have records with a view to be used in monetary calculations, use the currency information type, which plays calculations without rounding errors.)

The exact sort of numeric records stored in quite a number area is decided via the field size property. Design your tables very conservatively and permit for larger values than you ever assume to peer to your database. This isn't always to say that using the Double information type for all numeric fields is a good idea. The Double data type is very big (8 bytes) and is probably extremely slow when used in calculations or different numeric operations. Instead, the single data type might be best for most floating-point calculations, and long Integer is a great choice in which decimal points are irrelevant.

Large numbers

The large number data type holds values from -2^{63} to $2^{63}-1$. The ones are larger numbers than most of the people want. It turned into Access specially for compatibility with other databases which have this information type, in particular SQL Server.

In case you use massive range, be aware that not all variations of Access previous to 2019 support this data type. In case you're linking to or uploading from a database that makes use of this information type, take a look at support large range (Big Integer) facts type for connected/Imported Tables check container within the modern Database tab of access options.

Date/Time

The Date/Time statistics kind is a specialized range discipline for containing dates or times (or dates and instances). While dates are stored in a Date/Time subject, it's easy to calculate days between dates and different calendar operations. Date facts stored in Date/Time fields kind and filter properly as nicely. The Date/Time facts type holds dates from January 1, 100, to December 31, 9999.

Currency

The currency records kind is any other specialized number discipline. Currency numbers are not rounded throughout calculations and preserve 15 digits of precision to the left of the decimal factor and 4 digits to the proper. Because currency fields use a fixed decimal factor role, they're faster in numeric calculations than doubles.

Autonumber

The autonumber area is every other specialized variety data type. While an autonumber field is added to a table, access mechanically assigns a long integer (32-bit) value to the field (starting at 1) and increments the value every time a document is introduced to the table. Instead (determined by way of the new Values property), the cost of the autonumber subject is a random integer that is automatically inserted into new records.

Only one autonumber field can appear in a table. As soon as assigned to a report, the cost of an autonumber discipline can't be changed programmatically or by means of the user. Autonumber fields are stored as a protracted Integer facts type and occupy 4 bytes. Autonumber fields can accommodate as much as 4,294,967,296 specific numbers extra than adequate because the primary key for maximum tables.

Yes/No

Yes/No fields receive simplest considered one of two viable values. Internally saved as −1 (yes) or 0 (No), the yes/No field is used to indicate on/off, yes/no, or true/false. A yes/No area occupies a single bit of storage.

5.2 OLE object

The OLE object field stores OLE information, exceedingly specialized binary items inclusive of word files, Excel spreadsheets, sound or video clips, and pics. The OLE item is created via a software that windows acknowledges as an OLE server and can be connected to the figure software or embedded in the get right of entry to desk. OLE items may be displayed best in bound object frames in get admission to bureaucracy and reviews. OLE fields can't be indexed.

Hyperlink

The hyperlink records type field holds combinations of text and numbers saved as text and used as a link cope with. It is able to have as much as four parts:

The textual content that looks in a control (typically formatted to look like a clickable hyperlink).
The cope with—the course to a document or web page.
Any sub-cope with within the record or page. An instance of a sub-cope with is a image on
A web page. Each a part of the link's address is separated with the aid of the pound sign (#).
The text that looks in the display tip while the consumer hovers over the hyperlink.
MS Access hyperlinks may even point to forms and reviews in different MS Access to databases. Which means that you may use a hyperlink to open a form or report in an external Access database and show the form or document at the person's computer.

Attachment

The Attachment statistics kind became introduced in get admission to 2007. In truth, the Attachment statistics type is one of the motives Microsoft modified the format of the MS Access to information record. The older MDB format is not able to accommodate attachments.

The Attachment data type is relatively complicated, compared to the alternative styles of Access fields, and it calls for a unique form of manipulate whilst displayed on Access field.

Calculated

A Calculated field holds an expression that may include numbers, text, fields from within the same table, and Access features. It cannot reference fields from different tables. "Calculated" isn't a data type despite the fact that access consists of it within the information kind listing. It has a Result Type property that determines what kind of facts the field holds. You would possibly use a Calculated field if you find you're appearing the same calculations in queries time and again. For instance, if you had a Taxable Amount field and a Sales Tax Rate field, you could create a Sales Tax Amount subject that multiplies them together.

The use of this field comes dangerously close to violating the third normal form. The field virtually shops the system and not the calculated price. However, this is what queries are for and you could locate that maintaining the information to your tables and the calculations in your queries is a good manner to organize your software application.

Lookup Wizard

The lookup Wizard data type inserts a subject that enables the end user to choose a value from every other table or from the results of a SQL statement. The values can also be supplied as a blend box or list box. At design time, the lookup Wizard leads the developer through the procedure of defining the research characteristics when this information is assigned to a field. As you drag an object from the lookup Wizard area list, a combo box or listing field is automatically created at the form. The listing box or mixture field also seems on a query datasheet that incorporates the field.

Chapter 6

6.1 Changing table design/layout

Even the high-quality planned table may additionally require changes now and again. You may find which you need to feature any other field, change a name of the field, exchange a field name or data type, or in reality rearrange the order of the fields names.

Although a table's layout can be modified at any time, special issues ought to accept to tables containing facts. Be careful of making adjustments that harm data in the table, which include making textual content fields smaller or converting the filed size belongings of range fields. You can constantly add new fields to a table without issues, but changing existing fields is probably a problem. And, with only a few exceptions, it's almost always an awful concept to change a field's name after a table has been positioned into use in an application.

Insertion of new field

To insert a new field, inside the tale design window, place your cursor on a current field, proper click on an area within the table design surface, and select Insert Rows, or just click the Insert Rows button on the layout tab of the Ribbon. A new row is added to the table, and current fields are driven pushed down. You could then input a new field definition. Inserting a field doesn't disturb different fields or present facts. When you have queries, forms, or reports that use the table, you may want to add the field to the ones objects as properly.

Deleting a field

There are three methods to delete a field. Even as the table is in design view:

- Pick the field by means of clicking the row selector and then press Delete.
- Right-click on the chosen field and choose Delete Rows from the shortcut menu.
- Select the field and click on the Delete Rows button from the equipment group on the
Design tab of the Ribbon.

When you delete a field containing any data, you'll see a warning that you'll lose crucial data in the table for the selected in a field. If the table includes data, make sure which you want to eliminate the data for that field (column). You'll additionally should delete the identical field from queries, bureaucracy, reports, macros, and VBA code that use the field name.

In case you deleting a field, you must also fix all references to that area all through access. Due to the fact you could use a subject call in paperwork, queries, reports, and even table information validation, you should examine your gadget carefully to locate any instances in that you would possibly have used the precise field name.

Changing field location

The order of your fields, as entered inside the table layout view, determines the left to proper column collection inside the table's Datasheet view. If making a decision that your fields need to be rearranged, click on a subject selector and use the mouse to pull the sphere to its new area.

Converting a field name

You change a discipline's name by way of choosing the fields name within the table layout window and coming into a new name. Get right of entry to updates the table design routinely. As long as you're creating a new table, this process is straightforward. For current tables which can be referenced some other place in your software application, changing the field name can expose issues.

Changing field size

Creating a data size large is easy in a table layout. You definitely increase the field length belongings for text fields or specify an extraordinary subject size for number fields. You need to take note of the Decimal places belongings in wide variety fields to make certain you don't pick a new size that helps fewer decimal locations than you currently have.

Chapter 7

7.1 Selecting data with queries

7.1.1 Introducing queries

The word query comes from the Latin phrase quaerere, which means that "to ask or inquire." Over time, the word question has turn out to be synonymous with quiz, project, inquire, or question.

An MS Access query is a question that you ask approximately the information saved in Access tables. You buildup queries with the tools of MS access query. Your query may be a simple query about information in a single table, or it could be a greater complex query approximately information saved in numerous tables. As an example, you would possibly ask your database to expose you best vehicles that have been bought within the year of 2012. After you publish the query inside the shape of a question, Access returns most effective the data you have requested.

Creating query

When you create your tables and place records in them, you're able to work with queries. To begin a question, select the Create tab at the Ribbon, and click on the question layout button within the Queries organization. The underlying window is the question dressmaker. Floating on top of the query designer is the show table dialog box. The display table dialog field is modal, this means that which you ought to do something in the conversation container before continuing with the question. Earlier than you keep, you add the tables required for the question. In this example, tblproducts is highlighted and prepared to be added.

Figure # 7.1

The Show Table dialog box and the query design window.

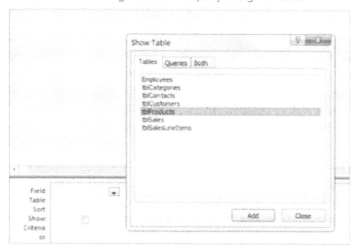

Getting rid of a table from the query is easy. Virtually right-click on the table within the question query designer and pick out dispose of table from the shortcut menu.

The query layout window has three primary views:

- Layout view: wherein you create the query
- Datasheet view: presentations the statistics again by the question
- SQL view: presentations the sq. Statement in the back of a question

The query designer consists of two sections:

- **The table/query pane:** this is in which tables or queries and their respective discipline lists are brought to the query's layout. You'll see a separate field listing for every item to add. Every field list includes the names of all the fields inside the respective table or query. You may resize a field listing by means of clicking the rims and dragging it to a special length. You can need to resize a field list so that each one of a table's fields are seen.

Figure # 7.2

The query design window with tblProducts added.

- **The query via layout (QBD) grid:** The QBD grid holds the field names Involved in the query and any criteria used to pick data. Each column within the

QBD grid incorporates facts about a single field from a table or query contained

Inside the top pane.

The QBD grid has six labeled rows:

- **Field:** this is in which field names are entered or delivered.

- **Table:** This row suggests the table the field in the table is from. That is beneficial in queries with multiple tables.
- **Sort:** This row enables sorting commands for the queries in the table or field.
- **Show:** This row determines whether to show the field inside the returned record set.
- **Criteria:** This row includes the criteria that clear out the lower back records.
- **Or:** This row is the first of a number of rows to which you could add a couple of query standards.

The query tools design Ribbon incorporates many buttons precise to building and working with queries. Even though each button is explained.

Figure # 7.3

The Query Tools Design Ribbon.

- **View:** Switches among the Datasheet view and design view within the question layout window. The View drop down control additionally enables you to show the underlying SQL statement in the back of the query.
- **Run:** Runs the query. Shows a select question's datasheet, serving the same function as choosing Datasheet View from the View button. However, whilst running with action queries, the Run button performs the operations (append, make table, and so on) detailed with the aid of the question.
- **Select:** Clicking the select button transforms the opened question into a choose query.

- **Make table, Append, replace, Crosstab, and Delete:** each of those buttons specifies the type of question you're building. In most instances, you transform a pick question into a movement question by way of clicking one of these buttons.
- **Display table:** Opens the display desk dialog container.

Chapter 8

8.1 Joins

You'll often want to build queries that require or greater related tables to be joined to achieve the desired results. As an instance, you could need to enroll in a worker table to a transaction table in order create a record that incorporates both transaction details and information at the personnel who logged into those transactions. The sort of join used will decide the information a good way to be output.

Getting to know joins

There are three basic varieties of joins: inner joins, left outer joins, and right outer joins.

Inner joins: An internal join operation tells Access to pick handiest those data from each tables that have matching values in both tables. Facts with values inside the joined field that don't seem in both tables are neglected from the query effects.

An inner join operation will choose simplest the data which have matching values in each tables. The arrows point to the information that will be included within the consequences.

Figure # 8.1

Left outer joins: A left outer join operation (on occasion known as a "left be a part of") tells get entry to pick all the data from the primary table regardless of if the data matches or not in the second table that have matching values within the joined operation virtually.

A left outer be part of operation will pick out all information from the primary table and simplest those data from the second table that have matching values in each tables. The arrows factor to the facts with the intention to be blanketed in the effects.

Figure # 8.2

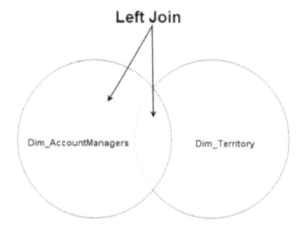

Right outer joins: A right outer join (once in a while known as a "right join" just) tells get Access to choose all the data from the second one table no matter matching and most effective the ones records from the primary table that have matching values inside the joined subject.

A right outer join Access all the information from the second one table and handiest those data from the first table that have matching values in both tables. The arrows point to the records to be able to be included within the results.

Figure # 8.3

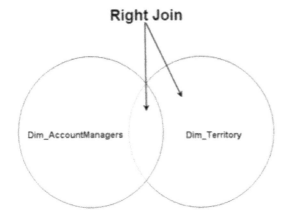

By means of default, an Access query returns most effective information where information exists on both aspects of a relationship (inner join). As an instance, a query that extracts data from the Contacts table and the income table only returns facts where contacts have sincerely located income and will no longer display contacts who haven't yet placed a sale. If a contact record isn't matched with the aid of at least one income file, the touch facts isn't back by means of the query. Which means that, occasionally, the query won't return all of the records you assume. Despite the fact that that is the maximum commonplace be part of kind among tables in a query, users every so often want to peer all of the data in a table regardless of whether those data are matched in another table. In reality, users frequently need to mainly see records that aren't matched on the alternative side of the join. Do not forget a sales branch that desires to recognize all the contacts that have no longer made a sale inside the last year. You should regulate the default question join characteristics on the way to process this form of query.

You can create joins between tables in those three approaches:

- By using growing relationships between the tables whilst you design the database.
- By using deciding on two tables for the query which have a subject in common that has the same call and information type in both tables. The field is a primary key field in one in all the tables.
- By way of enhancing the default be a part of behavior.

The first two methods occur robotically inside the query design window. Relationships among tables are displayed in the query designer while you add the related tables to a query. It additionally creates an automatic join between tables that have a not unusual area, so long as that field is a primary key in one of the tables and the allow Autojoin preference is chosen (by using default) inside the alternatives conversation field.

If relationships are set inside the Relationships window, you may not see the autojoin if:

- The two tables have a common subject; however, it isn't the same call.
- A desk isn't associated and mayn't be logically associated with the opposite table (for example, tblcustomers can't at once be part of the tblsaleslineitems table).

When you have two tables that aren't associated and also you need to enroll in them in a query, use the query layout window. Becoming a member of tables within the query layout window does no longer create a permanent relationship among the tables; as an alternative, join relationship applies most effective to the tables even as the query operates.

Chapter 9

9.1 Operators and Expressions

9.1.1 Introducing the operators

Operators permit you to evaluate values, positioned textual content strings together, layout data, and carry out an extensive variety of duties. You use operators to train access to perform a specific action against one or extra operands. The combination of operators and operands is known as an expression. You'll use operators each time you create an equation in get entry to. For instance, operators specify statistics validation rules in desk homes, create calculated fields in bureaucracy and reviews, and specify standards in queries.

9.2 types of operators

Operators can be grouped into the subsequent types:

- Comparison
- Boolean (logical)
- Miscellaneous
- String
- Mathematical

9.2.1 Mathematical operators

Mathematical operators are also known as mathematics operators, due to the fact they're used for appearing numeric calculations. By definition, you use mathematical operators to paintings with numbers as operands. When you work with mathematical operators, numbers can be any numeric facts kind. The range may be a steady fee, the value of a variable, or a field's contents. You operate these numbers individually or combine them to create complex expressions.

There are seven primary mathematical operators:

+ Addition
− Subtraction
* Multiplication
/ department
\ Integer department ^ Exponentiation Mod Modulo

Addition Operator

For calculated fields in a query.

[tax amount] + [price]

Subtraction Operator

[Amount] + [Amount] * [Discount percentage]

Multiplication Operator

To calculate the total price of several items having same price.

[price] * [Quantity of product]

Division Operator

To determine the individual persons payoff.

21 / 3

Exponentiation Operator

Raise number to the power of the exponent.

4 x 4 x 4 that is 4^3

9.2.2 Comparison operators

Contrast operators evaluate two values or expressions in an equation. There are six fundamental assessment operators:

= equal
<> not equal
< less than
<= less than or identical to
> greater than
>= greater than or equal to

Equal operator

This operator returns true if both of the expressions are same.

[category] = "Audi" returns true if category is Audi otherwise will return false.

Not equal operator

[category] < > "Audi" returns true if the category is anything but Audi.

9.2.3 String operators

There are three types of string operators.

- Concatenates operand &
- Operands are similar LIKE
- Operands are dissimilar NOT LIKE

9.2.4 Boolean operators

Boolean operators (additionally referred to as logical operators) are used to create multiple conditions in expressions. Like comparison operators, these operators constantly return false, true, or Null. Boolean operators consist of the subsequent:

- And returns true whilst both Expression1 and Expression2 are true.
- Or returns true when either Expression1 or Expression2 is true.
- Not returns true while the Expression isn't true.
- Xor returns true whilst both Expression1 or Expression2 is authentic, however now not both.
- Eqv returns true whilst both Expression1 and Expression2 are authentic or each are

False.

- Imp performs bitwise comparisons of identically placed bits in two numerical

Expressions.

Chapter 10

10.1 Aggregate Queries

An aggregate query, sometimes referred to as a collection by means of query, is a sort of query you may construct to help you quick congregate into group and summarize your data. With a select query, you may retrieve records most effective as they seem to your facts source. But with an aggregate query, you may retrieve a summary snapshot of your facts that indicates you totals, averages, counts, and greater.

Create aggregate query

To get a company understanding of what an aggregate query does, don't forget the following scenario: You've simply been requested to offer the sum of general sales with the aid of length. In response to this request, begin a question in layout view and bring in the Dim Dates period and Dim Transactions. Line Total fields, as proven in figure 10.1. If you run this query as is, you'll get every record to your information set in preference to the precis you want.

Figure # 10.1

Running this query will return all the records in your data set, not the summary you need.

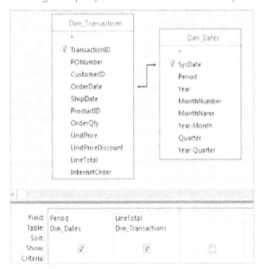

So, one can get a price of sales by means of duration, you'll need to set off Totals to your layout grid. To do that, go to the Ribbon and pick the layout tab, and then click on the Totals button. As you can see in figure 10.2, when you've activated Totals on your layout grid, you'll see a new row on your grid called total. The overall row tells access which aggregate feature to apply when appearing aggregation on the desired fields.

Word that the entire row consists of the phrases group by using under every field on your grid. Because of this all comparable records in a field might be grouped to provide you with a unique records object. The concept right here is to modify the combination capabilities inside the total row to correspond with the analysis you're trying to perform. In this state of affairs, you want to organization all of the intervals to your records set and then sum the revenue in each period. Consequently, you'll need to use the group by aggregate feature for the duration discipline, and the Sum aggregate feature for the Line Total field. Because the default selection for Totals is the group by using feature, no alternate is needed for the length discipline. But, you'll need to alternate the aggregate characteristic for the Line Total subject from institution by means of Sum. This tells Access which you need to sum the sales figures within the Line Total field, not group them. To trade the aggregate feature, truly click the entire drop-down listing beneath the Line Total subject, shown in figure 10.3, and pick out Sum. At this factor, you could run your query.

Figure # 10.2

Activating Totals in your design grid adds a Total row to your query grid that defaults to Group By.

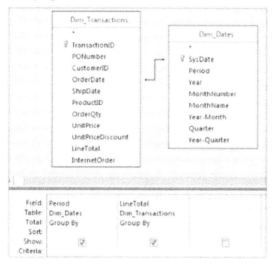

Figure # 10.3

Change the aggregate function under the LineTotal field to Sum.

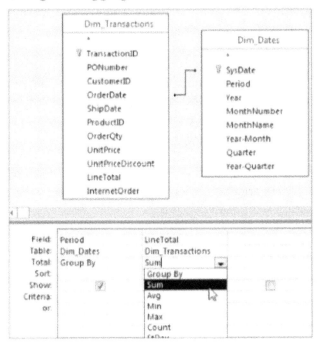

Figure # 10.4

Period	SumOfLineTotal
201107	$1,282,530.35
201108	$3,008,547.90
201109	$2,333,985.05
201110	$1,982,360.35
201111	$4,338,025.75
201112	$3,457,253.40
201201	$1,928,725.30
201202	$3,712,032.10
201203	$3,109,211.70
201204	$2,224,498.50
201205	$4,308,999.75

9.2 Group By

The group by aggregate function all the records in the specified area into particular organizations. Here are some things to hold in thoughts while the usage of the group by through the aggregate functions:

- **Access performs the** Group by using function in your mixture query earlier than every other aggregation. In case you're acting a group with the aid of at the side of some other aggregate characteristic, the Group by the aid of function will be proffered first. MS Access it just groups the period field first then summing the line total field

- **MS Access sorts every group by the fields in ascending order.** Until otherwise distinct, any area tagged as a set via field tagged as group by in ascending order. In case your query has a couple of group by using fields, each subject can be sorted in ascending order starting with the leftmost discipline.

- **Access treats a couple of group by fields as one unique item.** This question counts all of the transactions that have been logged within the 201201 length.

9.3 Sum, Avg, rely, stdev, Var

Those combination capabilities all perform mathematical calculations against the records in your chosen discipline. It's essential to notice that those capabilities exclude any statistics that are set to null. In different words, these mixture functions forget about any empty cells.

Sum: Calculates the full value of all the records inside the certain subject or grouping. This characteristic will work best with the subsequent information types: autonumber, currency, Date/Time, and number.

Avg: Calculates the average of all of the data inside the targeted designated or grouping. This feature will paintings most effective with the following information kinds: autonumber, currency, Date/Time, and wide variety.

Count: Counts the quantity of entries within the distinct field or grouping. This feature works with all data types.

Stdev: Calculates the same old deviation throughout all records inside the distinctive discipline or grouping. This characteristic will paintings best with the following records kinds: autonumber, Currency, Date/Time, and number.

Var: Calculates the amount via which all the values within the detailed field or grouping vary from the average cost of the group. This feature will work handiest with the subsequent data types: autonumber, currency, Date/Time, and variety.

9.4 Min, Max, First, last

Unlike different mixture capabilities, these features examine all of the facts in the special area or grouping and go back a single cost from the group.

Min: Returns the price of the file with the bottom cost inside the distinctive field or grouping. This function will work only with the following facts types: autonumber, currency, Date/Time, number, and textual content.

Max: Returns the price of the file with the maximum value in the record or column grouping. This characteristic will work most effective with the subsequent facts types: autonumber, forex, Date/Time, range, and textual content.

First: Returns the price of the first record inside the specific column or grouping. This function works with all kinds of data types.

Last: Returns the value of the remaining file in the precise field or grouping. This function works with all data types.

9.5 Expression where

One of the steadfast guidelines of aggregate queries is that each area ought to have an aggregation carried out in opposition to it. But, in some conditions you'll must use a subject as a utility that is, use a field to simply carry out a calculation or apply a clear out. Those fields are a means to get to the final evaluation you're looking for, as opposed to part of the final analysis. In those situations, you'll use the Expression characteristic or the where clause. The Expression feature and the in which clause are precise in that they don't carry out any grouping action per se.

Expression: The Expression combination feature is normally carried out whilst you are making use of custom calculations or other features in a mixture question. Expression tells access to carry out the specified custom calculation on every character record or organization one.

Where: The where clause lets in you to apply a criterion to a discipline that is not blanketed for your combination question, efficaciously making use of a clear out in your analysis.
Note which you're using aliases on this question: "revenue" for the Line Total subject and "fee" for the custom calculation defined here. The usage of an alias of "revenue" gives the sum of Line Total a user pleasant name.

Chapter 11

11.1 MS Access Macros

Macros have been part of access on account that the start. As get right of entry to developed as a development tool, the visual primary for applications (VBA) programming language have become the same old in automating MS Access database applications. Macros in versions previous to access 2007 lacked variables and mistakes handling, which precipitated many developers to desert macros altogether. Get entry to nowadays has those, which make macros a much more possible alternative to VBA than in preceding versions. If you're developing a database to be used on the web, or if you aren't a VBA guru however you continue to want to personalize the movements that your utility executes, then constructing based macros is the solution.

Introduction to Macros

A macro is a tool that allows you to automate responsibilities in Access database. It's distinctive from word's Macro Recorder, which helps you to record a chain of actions and play them returned later. (It's additionally distinctive from phrase in that phrase macros are sincerely VBA code, whereas access macros are something very special.) Access macros allow you to carry out defined moves and upload capability on your forms and reviews. Think of macros as a simplified, step cleared programming language. You build a macro as a list of movements to carry out, and you make a decision while you need those movements to arise. Constructing macros consists of choosing actions from a drop-down listing and then filling in the motion's arguments (values that offer facts to the movement). Macros allow you to pick actions without writing a single line of VBA code. The macro actions are a subset of commands VBA presents. The majority find it less difficult to construct a macro than to write VBA code. In case you're no longer acquainted with VBA, constructing macros is a notable stepping stone to studying some of the instructions available to you at the same time as providing brought fee to your get admission to programs. Suppose you need to construct a primary shape with buttons that open the alternative forms for your utility. You can add a button to the form, construct a macro that opens some other form in your software, after which assign this macro to the button's click occasion. The macro may be a standalone item that looks inside the Navigation pane, or it is able to be an embedded item that is part of the event itself.

Creating Macro

An easy manner to demonstrate a way to create macros is to build one which shows a message box that says, "hello world" To create a new stand by standalone macro, click the Macro button at the Macros & Code organization on the Create tab of the Ribbon.

Figure # 11.1

Use the Macro button on the Create tab to build a new stand-alone macro.

Clicking the Macro button opens the macro builder. To start with, the macro builder is nearly featureless. The best component in the Macro Builder is a drop-down list of macro moves.

To the proper of the Macro Builder you could see the movement Catalog. There are dozens of different macro moves and knowing which motion to apply for a selected mission can be an issue. The action Catalog provides a tree view of all to be had macro movements and allows you understand which action is wanted to perform a selected task. Select Message Box from the drop-down listing in the macro builder. The macro builder changes to show a place wherein you enter the arguments

(Message, Beep, type, and name) related to the Message Box motion.

Set the arguments as follows:

- **Message:** hello world!
- **Beep:** No
- **Type:** None
- **Name:** A simple Macro

Figure # 11.2

The macro builder displaying the Macro Builder and Action Catalog.

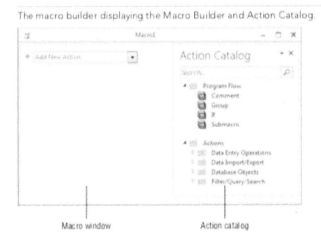

Macro window   Action catalog

The Message argument defines the textual content that appears in the message box and is the best argument that is required and has no default. The Beep argument determines whether or not a beep is heard whilst the message container appears. The sort argument sets which icon appears inside the message box: None, essential, caution?, warning!, or facts. The title argument defines the textual content that looks in the message container's title bar.

Figure # 11.3

The Hello World! macro uses the MessageBox action to display a message.

To run the macro, click the Run button within the tools institution of the layout tab of the Ribbon. (The Run button seems like a large purple exclamation factor on a ways left of the Ribbon.) When you create a new macro or trade an existing macro, you'll be triggered to save the macro. In reality, you have to save the macro before access runs it for you. When caused, click sure to store it, provide a name (such as "macros helloworld"), and click on adequate. The macro runs and dis- plays a message field with the arguments you special.

Figure # 11.4

Running the Hello World! macro displays a message box.

You could also run the macro from the Navigation pane. Close the macro builder and display the Macros group in the Navigation pane. Double-click the macros helloworld macro to run it. You'll see the identical message field that displayed when you ran the macro from the design window. Note that the message container constantly seems close to the middle of the display screen and blocks you from working with Access until you click good enough. Those are integrated behaviors of the message container item and are same in each regard to a message field displayed from VBA code. Whilst you're satisfied with the hello world! Macro, click the near button within the top-right corner of the macro builder to go back to the Access window.

Chapter 12

12.1 Access VBA

Most Access developers macros now after which. Despite the fact that macros offer a brief and clean manner to automate an application, writing visible basic for packages (VBA) modules is the excellent way to create packages. VBA offers data Access, looping and branching, and different features that macros virtually don't assist or as a minimum not with the power most builders want. On this forms, you learn how to use VBA to extend the energy and value of your applications.

12.2 Introducing visual simple

Visual basic for packages (VBA) is the programming language built into Microsoft Access. VBA is shared amongst all the workplace office applications, which includes Excel, word, Outlook, PowerPoint, and even Visio. In case you aren't already a VBA programmer, getting to know the VBA syntax and a way to hook VBA into the Access occasion version is a definite career builder. VBA is a key element in maximum professional Access applications. Microsoft presents VBA in access due to the fact VBA provides huge flexibility and power to Access database applications. Without a full composed programming language like VBA, access packages might ought to rely upon the truly restricted set of actions supplied by means of Access macros. Despite the fact that macro programming also provides flexibility to access applications, VBA is a good deal easier to paintings with whilst you're programming complex records management functions or sophisticated person interface necessities. In case you're new to programming, attempt not to come to be frustrated or crushed by way of the seeming complexity of the VBA language. As with all new skill, you are much higher off approaching VBA programming by using taking it one step at a time. You need to study exactly what VBA can do for you and your packages, at the side of the overall syntax, announcement shape, and the way to compose procedures using the VBA language.

Chapter 13

13.1 Integration of Microsoft Access with SharePoint

SharePoint is Microsoft's collaborative server environment, providing equipment for sharing files and statistics throughout numerous groups inside your company network. SharePoint is typically deployed on an organization's network as a series of SharePoint web sites. A SharePoint website is configured as an intranet site, giving diverse departments the ability to govern their personal safety, workgroups, documents, and facts. Those web sites can be nested within different websites in a hierarchical style. As with any other website, the pages inside a SharePoint site are available via a URL that the person can get entry to via a well-known web browser. Although SharePoint is maximum regularly used for sharing files, records tables, and other content control responsibilities, SharePoint is often carried out many other applications as an instance, to address the documentation required for product improvement. A SharePoint web site committed to improvement mission easily handles the challenge initiation, monitoring, and development reporting tasks. Due to the fact SharePoint without problems handles sincerely any type of document, mission drawings, motion pictures, schematics, snap shots, and so on, may be delivered to the task's SharePoint web site for overview and remark by means of venture contributors.

Companies regularly use SharePoint for dispensing human aid and coverage documents. Because SharePoint offers user and institution degree safety, it's pretty clean to supply a particular branch access to a SharePoint page at the same time as denying different users access to the same web page. SharePoint also logs changes to files and supports a take a look check in/check out paradigm for controlling who is eligible to make modifications to current documents and who's allowed to post new files and files.

Conclusion

MS access has a lot of advantages over other database and it provides you with certain benefits if you have designed the data base really well **Prevention of Human error** MS Access catches inconsistencies caused by human blunders. As an example, your group may additionally have entered the equal patron below distinctive names via accident. (suppose "Grand Rapids Heating & Plumbing" vs. "Grand Rapids Heating"). Whilst this takes place, it is tough to drag all of the information you need for a purchaser. Microsoft Access to prevents those kinds of human errors. **Create person Interfaces** The "consumer interface" is the display screen your personnel will see after they input or edit records. In Access, you are able to create paperwork that simplest show the fields important for employees to do their jobs. This also gives your company better facts security. That way, your employees don't have complete get right of entry to on your corporation records. **Proportion Your Findings** certain sorts of records can tell your enterprise decisions transferring ahead. For instance, you may need to look what number of new leads you've got gotten after an advertising marketing campaign. One of the most important benefits of Microsoft Access to is that it is simple to proportion your findings with others. While you make a document in Microsoft access, you may print, export, or email it to other participants of your crew. That way, you'll be capable of share your findings and collaborate quite simply.

C++

The Beginners Guide To Learn C++
Programming Step-by-Step
By Robert Coding

Introduction

C++ is a for the most part significant programming language proposed to make programming more charming for the authentic software engineer. With the exception of minor subtleties, C++ is a superset of the C programming language. In spite of the working environments given by C, C++ gives adaptable and fruitful work environments to depicting new sorts. A softwareengineer can disperse application into sensible pieces by depicting new sorts that enthusiastically match the musings of the application. This technique for program construction is routinely called information thought. Objects of some client depicted sorts contain type data. Such things can be utilized well and securely in settings in which their sortcan't be hinder mined at arrange time. Adventures utilizing objects of such sorts are constantly called object based. Right when utilized well, these situations accomplish more confined, more plainly obvious, and simpler to really focus on programs.

The significant idea in C++ is class. A class is a client depicted sort. Classes give up informationcovering, ensured instatement of information, seen sort change for client depicted sorts, dynamic shaping, client-controlled memory the heads, and instruments for over-upsetting chiefs. C++ gives much better work environments to type checking and for passing on separation than C does. It's like way contains upgrades that are not immediate identified with classes, including significant constants, inline substitution of cutoff points, default work clashes, over-inconvenience work names, free store the boss's administrators, and a reference type. C++ holds C's capacity to manage the central objects of the equipment (bits, bytes, words, addresses, and so on) This permits the client portrayed sorts to be executed with an awesome level of ability. C++ is an intermediate level language, as it contains a confirmation of both unquestionable level and low-level language features. C++ is a free form,statically type, multiparadigm, compiled general purpose language. C++ is an Object-Oriented Programming language at some points isn't totally Object Oriented. Its features like Friend and Virtual, contradict a bit of the essential OOPS features. Hence you can call it both an intermediate programming language as well as object-oriented programming language. C++ and its standard libraries are expected for portability. The current execution will run on most systems that help C. C libraries can be used from a C++ program, and most instruments that

Chapter 1

1.1 Description

C++, as we know in general is a wing to C language and was made by Bjarne Stroustrup at belllabs. C++ was intended to give Simula's working environments to program relationship close by C's ability and flexibility for structures programming. It was needed to give that to credibletasks inside a colossal section of a time of the thought.

The objective was really simple at thattime it didn't involve any sort of innovation and was quite a compromise on the flexibility andefficiency of the language. While an unassuming degree of progress emerged all through theextended length, efficiency and flexibility have been kept up without deal. While, the destinations for C++ have been refined, clarified, and made all the more express all through the long haul, C++ as used today clearly reflects its exceptional focuses. Most effort has been utilized on the early years because the arrangement decisions taken early chose the further improvement of the language. It is also less complex to keep an unquestionable perspective when one has had various years to see the aftereffects of decisions.

In this short book we will talk about how C++ language emerged over the time and what type of programming updates have occurred over the years.

Chapter 2

2.1 First Programming Language (Simula)

2.1.1 History

The essential object-oriented programming language was made during the 1960s at the Norwegian Registering Center in Oslo, by two Norwegian PC specialists—Ole-Johan Dahl (1931-2002) and Kristen Nygaard (1926-2002).

Kristen Nygaard, a MS in number juggling at the College of Oslo, started creating PC entertainment programs in 1957. He was searching for a better strategy than depict the heterogeneity and the movement of a system. To go further with his contemplations on an ordinary scripting language for depicting a system, Nygaard comprehended that he required someone with more PC programming capacities than he had, thusly he arrived at Ole-Johan Dahl, in like manner a MS in math and one of the Norway's chief PC analyst, who obliged him in January 1962.

In 1966 the English PC scientist Tony Hoare introduced record class create, which Dahl and Nygaard connected with prefixing and various features to meet their necessities for another summarized measure thought. The essential customary importance of Simula 67 appeared inMay 1967. In June 1967 a gathering was held to standardize the language and start differentexecutions. Dahl proposed to unite the sort and the class thought. This provoked real discussions, and the suggestion was excused by the board. SIMULA 67 was formally standardized on the chief fulfilling of the SIMULA Rules Gathering in February 1968.

Simula 6 contained huge quantities of the thoughts that are presently open in standard Object-oriented like Java, C++, and C#.

2.2 C++ Language evolution

The C++ programming language has a bunch of encounters getting back to 1979, when Bjarne Stroustrup was handling position for his Ph.D. Proposition. One of the vernaculars Stroustrupgot the opportunity to work with was a language called Simula, which as the name recommends is a language essentially proposed for reenactments. The Simula 67 language - which was the variety that Stroustrup worked with - is seen as the vital language to help the article masterminded programming perspective. Stroustrup found that this perspective was outstandingly important for programming improvement, in any case the Simula language was nonsensically postponed for sensible use.

2.3 C with classes

"C with Classes" was the earlier version of C++. C++ got evolved through it. The main purposeof C with classes was to add classes in to the language. This work happened in between 1979-1983. This work determines the shape of C++.

The work, on what finally became C++, started with an undertaking to analyze the UNIX partto choose the amount it might be passed on over an association of laptops related by an area.This work started in April of 1979 in the Figuring Science Exploration Focus of bell Labs in Murray Slope, New Jersey, the started forward. Two subproblems after a short time emerged: how to examine the association traffic that would result from the piece movement and how to modularize the part. Both required a way to deal with impart the module plan of a perplexing structure and the correspondence illustration of the modules. This was overall such an issue that had become concluded never to attack again without real instruments. Consequently, the development of a genuine contraption according to the models that wereoutlined in Cambridge.

During the April to October period the advancement from thinking about a "gadget" to contemplating a "language" had occurred, yet C with Classes was at this point considered ona very basic level as a growth to C for conveying estimated quality and synchronization. A fundamental decision had been made, notwithstanding. Notwithstanding the way that help of concurrence and Simula-style reenactments was a fundamental place of C with Classes, thelanguage contained no locals for imparting concurrence; rather, a mix of heritage (class levelsof leadership) and the ability to portray class part works with outstanding ramifications saw by the preprocessor was used to create the library that maintained the ideal styles of synchronization. Mercifully note that "styles" is plural. I considered it basic, as I really do, thatmore than one thought of concurrence should be expressible in the language. This decision has been reconfirmed more than once by me and my partners, by other C++ customers, andby the C++ standards warning gathering. There are various applications for which maintain for concurrence is principal, yet there is no one winning model for synchronization maintain; hence when sponsorship is required it should be given through a library or a particular explanation increase with the objective that a particular sort of concurrence maintain doesn'thinder various constructions.

As such, the language gave general instruments to figuring everything out programs instead of help for express application zones. This was what made C with Classes, and later C++, an extensively valuable language rather than a C variety with expansions to help specific applications. A short time later, the choice between offering assistance for explicit applications or general thought frameworks, has come up more than once. Each time the decision has been to improve the reflection segments.

An early depiction of C with Classes was conveyed as a bell Labs particular report in April 1980[Stroustrup 1980a], and later in SIGPLAN Takes note. The SIGPLAN paper was in April 1982, followed by a more point by point Chime Labs specific report, "Adding Classes to the C Language: An Activity in Language Development" [Stroustrup 1982], that was thusly appropriated in Programming: Practice and Experience. These papers set a real model by portraying simply features that were totally executed and had been used. This was according to a long-standing act of bell Labs Figuring Science Exploration Center; that plan has been changed exactly where more openness about the inevitable destiny of C++ got expected to ensure a free and open conversation over the headway of C++ among its various non-AT&T customers.

C with Classes was explicitly expected to allow better relationship of activities; "estimation" was seen as an issue tended to by C. The expressing point was to facilitate with C in regard to run-time, code minimization, and data diminutiveness. In reality: someone once showed a three percent purposeful decrease in commonly run-time efficiency compared with C. This was seen as unsuitable and the overhead promptly disposed of. In like manner, to ensure design likeness with C and therefore avoid space overheads, no "housekeeping data" was placed in class objects.

Another critical concern was to avoid impediments on the space where C with Classes could be used. The ideal - - which was cultivated - was that C with Classes could be used for whatever C could be used for. This proposed that just as organizing with C in efficiency, C with Classes couldn't offer advantages to the impediment of disposing of "dangerous" or "revolting" features of C. This discernment/standard should be repeated habitually to people (rare C with Classes customers) who required C with Classes made safer by growing static sort checking according to early Pascal. The elective technique for giving "security," embeddings run-time checks for each and every dangerous action, was (and is) considered reasonable for investigating conditions, at this point the language couldn't guarantee such checks without leaving C with a huge advantage in run-reality viability. Hence, such checks were not given for C Classes, anyway C++ conditions exist that give such checks to examining. Besides, customers can, and do, implant run-time checks (revelations [Stroustrup 1991]) where required and sensible.

C allows low-level errands, for instance, bit control and picking between different sizes of entire numbers. There are furthermore workplaces, as unequivocal unchecked sort changes, for deliberately breaking the sort structure, C with Classes, and later C++, follow this path byholding the low-level and perilous features of C. Instead of C, C++ intentionally discards the need to use such features beside where they are basic and performs hazardous undertakings exactly at the explicit request of the programmer. As every programmer have different stylesand ways to write a program and most certainly every problem have many ways to solve it so the language should be developed in a way so as to encourage a programmer to write his style out with only essentials of language to follow.

Features that were included in 1980:

1. Friend classes
2. Derived classes
3. Constructors and destructors

4. Public/private access control
5. Type checking and conversion of function arguments
6. Friend classes
7. Call and return functions (Section 15.2.4.8)

The features that they included into the language during 1981

8. Overloading of assignment operator
9. Default argument
10. Inline function

Since a preprocessor was used for the execution of C with Classes, simply new features, thatis, features not present in C, ought to have been depicted and the full power of C was direct open to customers. Both of these perspectives were esteemed by then. Having C as a subset fundamentally reduced the assistance and documentation work required. This was generallyhuge because for a serious drawn-out period of time I did the total of the C with Classes andlater C++ documentation and sponsorship just as doing the experimentation, plan, andexecution. Having all C features open additionally ensured that no requirements introduced through inclination or nonappearance of foresight on my part would prevent a customer from getting features viably open in C. Typically, convey ability to machines supporting C was ensured. From the start, C with Classes was done and used on a DEC PDP/11, yet soon it wasported to machines, for instance, DEC, VAX, and Motorola 68000-based machines. C with Classes was at this point seen as a vernacular of C. In addition, classes were insinuated as "A Theoretical Information Type Office for the C Language" [Stroustrup 1980a]. Support for object-orchestrated composing PC programs was not ensured until the course of action of virtual limits in C++ in 1983 [Stroustrup 1984a].

Key design decisions of that time:

1. C with Classes follows Simula in permitting the designer to decide types from which factors(objects) can be made, rather than, say, the Modula approach of showing a module as a grouping of articles and limits. In C with Classes (as in C++), a class is a sort, this is a fundamental thought in C++.
2. The depiction of objects of the customer portrayed sort is fundamental for the class introduction. This has broad consequences. For example, it suggests that certifiable area components can be done without the use of free store (load store, dynamic store) or refuse grouping. It moreover infers that a limit ought to be recompiled; the depiction of a thing it uses clearly is changed.
3. Gather time access control is used to bind permission to the depiction. As is normally done,only the limits referred to in the class confirmation can use names of class people. People

(when in doubt work people) showed in the public interface, the assertions after the public: name, can be used by other code.

4. The full kind (tallying both the return type and the conflict kinds) of a limit, is demonstrated for work people. Static (request time) type checking relies upon this benevolent detail. This changed from C by then, where work conflict types were neither decided in interfaces nor checked in calls.

5. Limit definitions are usually designated "elsewhere" to make a class more like an interfacespecific than a lexical instrument for figuring everything out source code. This gathers that extraordinary. This implies that separate accumulation for class part abilities and their clientsis simple and the linker period generally utilized for C is adequate to help C++.

6. The function new () is a constructor, a function with an uncommon which intends to the compiler. Such functions outfitted guarantees around directions. In this model, the assuranceis that the constructor, perceived actually confusingly as another trademark, on the time is destined to be alluded to as to introduce each object of its class before the primary utilizationof the object.

7. Both pointers and non-pointer types are provided (as in every C and Simula).

Much of the further improvements of C with classes and C++ may be viewed as investigating the consequences of these design decisions, misusing their proper components, and makingup for the issues coming about because of their awful features. Many, besides in no way all, of the ramifications of those layout picks were perceived at that point; Stroustrup [1980a] is dated April 3, 1980. This level endeavors to make clear what changed into comprehended atthe time and bring suggestions to segments clarifying later effects and acknowledge.

2.4 Run-Time Efficiency

The initial version of C with classes did not provide inline functions to take in addition benefit of the supply the illustration. Inline functions had been quickly provided, even though. The general purpose for the creation of inline functions became fear that the cost of crossing a protection barrier would possibly reason people to chorus from the use of commands to coverrepresentation. Specially, Stroustrup [1982] observes that human beings had made records contributors public to avoid the function name overhead incurred with the useful resource ofa constructor for simple schooling wherein most effective one or two assignments are needed for initialization. The instantaneous reason for the inclusion of inline capabilities into C with classes turned into a venture that could not control to pay for feature call overhead for a fewcommands involved in actual-time processing.

Over time, issues along those strains grew into the C++

"precept" that it became not so sufficient to offer a function, it had to be supplied in a less pricey form. Maximum really, "low fee" grow to be seen as that means "low-priced on hardware were common among developers" in area of "much less luxurious to researchers with excessive-quit device," or "low-cost in a couple of years while hardware can be less expensive." C with classes was continuously considered as a few things to be used now or subsequent month in choice as studies project to supply something in multiple years, therefore. In lining changed into taken into consideration critical for the application of education and, therefore, the difficultyemerge as more a way to offer it than whether or how not to offer it. Two arguments receivedthe day for the belief of getting the programmer pick out which functions the compiler needto attempt to inline.

The compiler best knows quality if it's been programmed to inline and it has a notion of time/space optimization that agrees with mine. The alternative languages become that most effective "the subsequent release" could actually inline and it might achieve this consistent with an inner good judgment that a programmer couldn't successfully manipulate. To make matters worse, C (and therefore, C with lessons and later C++) has authentic separate compilation in order that a compiler never has get admission to greater than a small a part ofthis system. In lining a function for which you don't know the supply seems feasible given advanced linker and optimizer technology, but such era wasn't to be had at the time (and still isn't in maximum environments).

2.5 The Linkage Model

The issue of the way one after the other compiled applications are connected together is vitalfor any programming language and, to a degree, determines the capabilities the language can provide. One of the crucial influences at the development of C with instructions and C++ wasthe choice that

1. Separate compilation ought to be possible with traditional C/FORTRAN UNIX/DOS fashionlinkers.
2. Linkage must in precept be kind secure.
3. Linkage must no longer require any form of database (even though one will be used toenhance a given implementation).
4. Linkage to software fragments written in other languages which include C, assembler, andFORTRAN have to be clean and green.

C makes use of "header documents" to ensure constant separate compilation. Declarations of facts structure layouts, capabilities, variables, and constants are located in header files which might be commonly textually blanketed into each supply record that wishes the declarations. Consistency is ensured through putting adequate information in the header files and making sure that the header documents are continuously protected. C++ follows this model up to some extent.

The purpose that format information may be found in a C++ class statement (although it doesn't have to be, is to make sure that the declaration and use of proper local variables is straightforward and efficient. As an instance:

```
Void func( )
{
 S
t
a
c
k
s
;
I
n
t
c
;
S
.
p
u
s
h
(
'
h
'
)
;
C
=
s
.
p
```

```
o
p
(
)
;
}
```

Using the stack declaration, even a simple-minded C with lessons implementation can make certain that no need is fabricated from free shop for this situation, that the decision of dad (
) is in lined so that no function name overhead is incurred and that the non-in lined call of push ( ) can invoke a one by one compiled characteristic pop (). On this, C++ resembles Ada [Ichbiah 1979].

The concern for easy-minded implementations became partly a need due to the lack of assetsfor developing C with classes and partially a mistrust of languages and mechanisms that required "smart" strategies. An early components of a layout aim was that C with lessons "must be implementable without using an set of rules extra complicated than a linear seek."anyplace that rule of thumb turned into violated, as inside the case of feature overloading , it led to semantics that had been more complicated than each person felt at ease with and usually also to implementation headaches.

The intention--based totally on my Simula experience--became to design a language that would be easy sufficient to apprehend to attract customers and smooth sufficient to enforceto draw implementers. Only if a fairly simple implementation might be used by an enormouslynewbie user in a rather unsupportive programming surroundings to deliver code that as compared favorably with C code in improvement time, correctness, run-time velocity, and code length, ought to C with training, and later C++, anticipate to live to tell the tale in competition with C.

This changed into a part of a philosophy of fostering self-sufficiency among customers. The intention turned into continually and explicitly to develop neighborhood knowledge in all aspects of the use of C++. Most organizations should observe the exact opposite approach. They preserve customers dependent on offerings that generate sales for a critical assist company and/or consultant. In my view, this contrast is a deep cause for some of the variations between C++ and plenty of different languages.

The decision to work in the pretty primitive and nearly universally available framework of the C linking centers triggered the essential trouble that a C++ compiler must continually paintings with handiest partial records approximately a software. An assumption made about a software ought to likely be violated via a program written the next day in a few other language(inclusive of C, FORTRAN, or assembler) and related in probable after this system has commenced executing. This trouble surfaces in many contexts. It's far tough for an implementation to assure

1. That something is unique,
2. That (kind) information is constant,
3. That something is initialized.

In addition, C offers handiest and feeblest guide for the perception of separate name spacesin order that fending off name space pollutants by way of one at a time written program segments becomes a trouble. Over the years, C++ has tried to stand all of these demanding situations without departing from the essential model and generation that gives portability, but within the C with training days we simply relied on the C technique of header documents.Through the popularity of the C linker got here every other "principle" for the development of C++: C++ is just one language in a system and not a complete device. In different phrases, C++ accepts the function of a traditional programming language with a fundamental difference among the language, the running machine, and other vital elements of the programmer's international. This delimits the position of the language in a way this is difficultto do for a language, inclusive of Smalltalk or Lisp, that became conceived as an entire gadget or environment. It makes it critical that a C++ software fragment can name program fragments written in other languages and that a C++ software fragment can itself be referred to as by means of software fragments written in other languages. Being "just a language" additionally allows C++ implementations to gain immediately from equipment written for different languages.

The need for a programming language and the code written in it to be only a cog in a miles larger gadget is of maximum significance to most business customers, yet such co-existence with other languages and systems was apparently not a primary problem to most theoreticians, might-be perfectionists, and academic users. It was the main reason for the success of C++.

2.6 Static Type Checking

To keep the C code away from breaking, it turned into decided to allow the call of an undeclared feature and not carry out type checking on such undeclared features. This becameof path a main hollow in the type machine, and several attempts had been made to decreaseits importance because the foremost occurrence of programming errors before in the end, inC++, the hollow was closed by using creating a call of an undeclared characteristic unlawful. One simple commentary defeated all tries to compromise, and as a result keep a greater diploma of C compatibility: As programmers found out C with training, they misplaced the capacity to find run-time errors as a result of simple type errors. Having come to depend on the sort checking and type conversion furnished by means of C with instructions or C++, theylost the capacity to quickly locate the "silly mistakes" that creep into C packages via the lack of checking. Similarly, they didn't take the precautions towards such silly errors that exact C programmers take as a count of path. After all, "such errors do not take place in C with training." for that reason, as the frequency of run-time mistakes caused by uncaught argument kind mistakes is going down, their seriousness and the time needed to discover them goes up. The result turned into critically annoyed programmers worrying similarly tightening of the kind machine.

The maximum thrilling test with "incomplete static checking" became the method of permitting calls of undeclared features but noting the type of the arguments used in order that a consistency test will be completed when in addition calls have been visible. Whilst Walter brilliant many years later independently discovered this trick, he named it "auto prototyping," the usage of the ANSI C term prototype for a function assertion. The revel in turned into that auto prototyping stuck many mistakes and to begin with multiplied aprogrammer's self-belief within the type machine. However, on the grounds that regular errors and mistakes in a characteristic known as simplest once in a compilation had been now not stuck, auto prototyping ultimately destroyed programmer confidence within the type checker and precipitated a feel of paranoia even worse than that was witnessed in C or BCPLprogrammers.

C with lessons brought the notation f (void) for a characteristic f that takes no arguments as a comparison to f ( ) that in C announces a function that could take any quantity of arguments of any type with none type test. My users soon convinced me, but, that the f (void) notation wasn't very fashionable, and that having functions declared f ( ) be given arguments wasn't very intuitive. Consequently, the end result of the experiment changed into to have f ( ) suggest a characteristic f that takes no arguments, as any beginner might count on. It took support from each Doug mciiroy and Dennis Ritchie for me to build up braveness to make this damage from C. Most effective when they used the phrase abomination approximately f (void) did I dare provide f ( ) the apparent which means. However, to this day C's kind regulations are a great deal laxer than C++'s and any use of f ( ) as a characteristic statement between the Two languages is incompatible.

2.7 Syntax Problem

In C, the call of a shape, a "shape tag," should continually be preceded with the aid of the key-word struct. For instance

Struct buffer a;   /* 'struct' is vital in C */

In the context of C with classes, this had annoyance for some time as it made user-described kinds second kind residents syntactically. The call of a struct or a category is now a type call and requires no unique syntactic identity:

Buffer a;   // C++

The ensuing fights over C compatibility lasted for years.

2.8 Derived Classes

The C with classes concept becomes supplied without any shape of run-time support. In particular, the Simula (and C++) concept of a virtual function became missing. The reason for this turned into the purpose, of educating human beings how to use them and, even extra, the persuasion of people that a virtual feature is as green in time and area as an everyday characteristic, as usually used. Often human beings with Simula and Smalltalk revel innonetheless don't quite believe that until they've had the C++ implementation explained to them in element--and plenty of still harbor irrational doubts after that. Even without virtual capabilities, derived lessons in C with classes have been beneficial for constructing new statistics systems out of antique ones and for associating operations with the resulting sorts. In particular, as explained in Stroustrup [1980] and Stroustrup [1982], they allowed list lessons to be defined, and also task training.

In the absence of digital capabilities, a consumer may want to use gadgets of a derived elegance and treat base instructions as implementation info (only). Alternatively, a specific kind field may be introduced in a base class and used together with express kind casts. The previous approach changed into used for responsibilities where the user handiest sees particular derived venture classes and "the system" sees most effective the undertaking basetraining. The latter approach was used for diverse software instructions wherein, in impact, a base magnificence turned into used to put in force a variant report for a hard and fast of derived training. A great deal of the effort in C with instructions and later C++ has been to make certain that programmers need not write such code.

2.9 Protection Model

Function were made to be able to declare in public parts of the class or by specifying a function or a category as a friend. Initially, simplest instructions may be pals, consequently granting get right of entry to all member features of the friend magnificence, but later it turned into observed handy so that it will grant get right of entry to (friendship) to individual features. Specifically, it changed into found useful if you want to furnish get entry to global functions. A friendship declaration turned into seen as a mechanism much like that of one safety domain granting a study-write capability to some other.

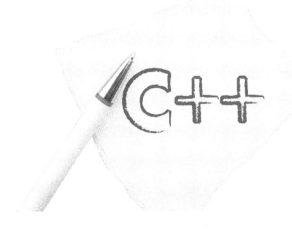

2.10 Run-Time Guarantees

The access control mechanisms defined above honestly prevent unauthorized get right of entry to. A second form of guarantee supplied by "special member features," which includesconstructors, that have been identified and implicitly invoked through the compiler. The idea was to permit the programmer to establish guarantees, once in a while called "invariants," that different member functions may want to rely upon. Curiously sufficient, the preliminary implementation contained a feature that isn't always provided via C++ but is regularly asked. In C with lessons, it became feasible to define a characteristic that might implicitly be known as earlier than each name of every member function (except the constructor) and another that might be implicitly referred to as earlier than every return from every member function. They were called call and return functions. They were used to provide synchronization for the monitor class inside the original task library [Stroustrup 1980b]:

Class monitor: object
{
/* ... */
C
a
l
l
(
)
(
/
*
p
i
c
k
l
o
c
k
*

```
/
)
R
e
t
u
r
n
(
)
(
.
/
*
r
e
l
e
a
s
e
l
o
c
k
*
/
)
}:
```

These are comparable in cause to the CLOS: before and: after methods. Name and return capabilities were eliminated from the language due to the fact no person used them and because no one persuaded human beings that call and return functions had essential uses. In 1987, Mike Tiemann cautioned an alternative solution known as "wrappers" [Tiemann 1987].

Chapter 3

3.1 From C with Classes to C++

Throughout 1982, it became clear that C with classes became a "medium success" and might remain so till it died. So, a medium was defined for fulfillment as something so beneficial that it without problems paid for itself and its developer, but not so attractive and beneficial that it'd pay for a help and improve organization. Accordingly, persevering with C with classes and its C preprocessor implementation would condemn to aid C with classes' use indefinitely. So, there were only two methods derived out of this dilemma:

1. Stop supporting C with classes, in order that the customers could need to pass elsewhere.

2. Develop a new and better language based on my experience with C with classes that would serve a huge sufficient set of users to pay for aid and development enterprise hence at that time it was observed that 5000 commercial users are essential minimum.

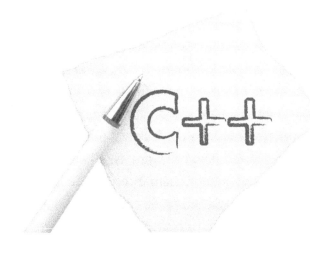

The success of C with classes became an easy outcome of assembly its layout purpose: C with instructions did help arrange a large elegance of applications considerably higher than C, without the lack of run-time performance and without requiring enough cultural adjustments to make its use unfeasible in groups that had been unwilling to undergo foremost changes. The elements restricting its success have been partially the limited set of latest facilities presented over C, and partially the preprocessor generation used to implement C with lessons. There simply wasn't sufficient assist in C with classes for individuals who have been willing to invest tremendous efforts to acquire matching advantages: C with classes become a vital step in the proper route, but simplest one small step.

The resulting language was at the start nonetheless referred to as C with lessons, however after a polite request from control it changed into given the name C84. The motive for the naming becomes that people had taken to calling C with classes "new C," after which C. This closing abbreviation caused C being known as "simple C," "immediately C," and "vintage C." The call C84 turned into used only for a few months, partially as it changed into unsightly andinstitutional, in part because there would nonetheless be confusion if humans dropped the "84." ideas for a brand-new call were asked and picked C++ because it became brief, had pleasant interpretations, and wasn't of the form "adjective C." In C, ++ can, depending on context, be examine as "next," "successor," or "increment," even though it's far usually suggested "plus". The call C++ and its runner up ++C are fertile assets for jokes and puns-- almost all of which had been regarded and favored before the name become chosen. The callC++ turned into cautioned by Rick Mascitti. It changed into first used in Stroustrup [1984b] wherein it become edited into the final copy in December 1983.

3.2 Cfront

The Cfront compiler front-end for the C84 language changed into designed and carried out via me between the spring of 1982 and the summer time of 983. The primary person outside the computer science research center, Jim Coplien, obtained his replica in July of 1983. Jim changed into in a group that were doing experimental switching paintings with C with Classesin Bell Labs in Naperville, Illinois, for some time.

In that equal time period designed C84, drafted the reference guide published January 1, 1984[Stroustrup 1984a], designed the complicated variety library and implemented it, collectively with Eeonie Rose[Rose]984], designed and implemented the first string class together with Jonathan Shopiro, maintained and ported the C with classes implementation, and supported the C with classes customers and helped them grow to be C84 users. Cfront turned into (and is) a traditional compiler the front-end, performing a whole take a look at of the syntax and semantics of the language, building an inner representation of its input, reading and rearranging that illustration, and subsequently producing output suitable for a few code generators. The internal illustration changed into (is) a graph with one symbol table in keeping with scope. The overall strategy is to study a supply document one worldwide statement at atime and bring output handiest when a whole global declaration has been completelyanalyzed.

The agency of Cfront is reasonably traditional, besides perhaps for the use of many symbol tables instead of just one. Cfront become at the beginning written in C with Classes and soon transcribed into C84 so that the very first running C++ compiler turned into executed in C++.Even the first model of Cfront used classes heavily, however no virtual capabilities because they were not available at the project start.

The maximum uncommon for its time issue of Cfront become that it generated C code. This has brought on no cease of confusion. Cfront generated C due to the fact. Ought to easily have generated some inner back-give up format or assembler from Cfront, however that turned into not what customers wanted. In reaction to this need, concluded that using C as a common input format to a massive variety of code turbines became the only reasonable preference. The strategy of constructing a compiler as a C generator has later become prettypopular, in order that languages consisting of Ada, CLOS, Eiffel, Modula-three, and Smalltalk have been applied that way. C compiler is used as a code generator most effective. Any mistakes message from the C compiler reflects a mistake inside the C compiler or in Cfront, however no longer within the C++ source textual content. Every syntactic and semantic blunder is in precept caught by usingCfront, the C++ compiler front-give up. There has been a protracted history of bewildermentabout what Cfront changed into/is. It's been known as a preprocessor because it generates C,and for humans within the C network (and some other place) that has been taken as evidencethat Cfront changed into an alternatively easy program something like a macro preprocessor.Humans have accordingly "deduced" (wrongly) that a line-for-line translation from C++ to C is possible, that symbolic debugging at the C++ level is impossible when Cfront is used, that code generated by using Cfront should be not so good as code generated with the aid of "actual compilers," that C++ wasn't a "actual language," and so on.

Cfront is just a compiler front-end and can by no means be used for real programming itself.It uses a driver force to run the source document through the C preprocessor, Cpp, then run the output of Cpp through Cfront, and the output from Cfront through a C compiler:

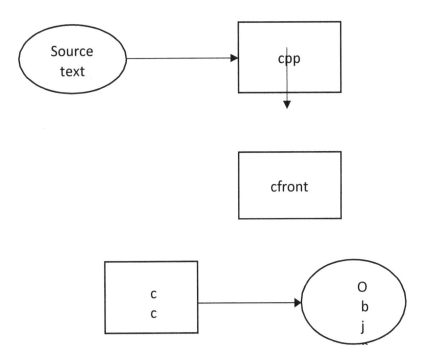

Similarly, the driver ought to make certain that dynamic (run-time) initialization is carried out. In Cfront 3.0, the driver became but extra intricate as automated template instantiation.

As stated, it was decided to stay within the constraints of traditional linkers. But there was one constraint that was felt too tough to live with: most traditional linkers had a very low restriction on the variety of characters that may be used in external names. A limit of 8 characters changed into not unusual, and 6 characters and one case most effective are guaranteed to work as outside names in Classical C; ANSI/ISO C accepts that restrict also. For the reason that the call of a member feature includes the name of its class and that the type of an overloaded characteristic needs to be meditated inside the linkage manner in some wayor other. Cfront uses encodings to enforce type safe linkage in a way that makes a restrictionof 32 characters too low for comfort and even 256 is a piece tight at instances. Within the meantime, systems of hash coding of long identifiers were used with archaic linkers, but that turned into by no means completely great.

Versions of C++ are often named by means of Cfront launch numbers. Launch 1.0 was the language as described in "The C++ Programming Language".

Releases 1.1 (June 1986) and 1.2 (February 1987) had been typically bug restoration releaseshowever also introduced hints to individuals and guarded contributors. Release 2.0 become a primary clean-up that still brought multiple inheritance in June 1989. Release 2.1 (April 1990) changed into more often than not a computer virus restore release that introduced Cfront (nearly) into line with the definition within the ARM. Release 3.0 (September 1991) delivered templates as detailed within the ARM. Launch 4.0 is predicted to feature exceptiondealing with as distinctive within the ARM.

3.3 Language Feature Details

1. References
2. Function name and operator overloading
3. Virtual functions
4. Improved type checking
5. User-controlled free-store memory control
6. Constants (const)

3.4 Virtual Functions

The most obvious new characteristic in C++, and clearly the one that had the finest impact onthe fashion of programming one should use for the language, was virtual functions. The idea become borrowed from Simula and presented in a shape that intended to make easy and efficient implementation.

The motive for virtual functions was presented in Stroustrup [1986b] and [1986c]. To emphasize the important position of virtual capabilities in C++ programming, i can be quote:"An abstract data type defines a form of black box. As soon as it's been described, it does nownot truly interact with the rest of the program. There's no way of adapting it to new uses except via modifying its definition. This could cause severe inflexibility. Keep in mind defininga type form for use in a portrait's device. Count on for the instant that the system has to aid circles, triangles, and squares. Expect additionally that you have a few classes:

C
l
a
s
s
p
o
i
n
t

/
*
.
.
.
*
/
)
;
C
l
a
s
s
c
o
l
o
r
/
*
.
.
.
*
/
;

You might outline a shape like this: Enum

```
kind (
circle,
triangle,
rectangula
r };Class
shape (
point
center;
Color col;
```

Kind k;
/
/
r
e
p
r
e
s
e
n
t
a
t
i
o
n
o
f
s
h
a
p
e
P
u
b
l
i
c
:

```
Point where () ( return center; }
Void move (point to)  {center = to; draw();
)
```

V
o
i
d
d
r
a
w
(
)
;
V
o
i
d
r
o
t
a
t
e
(
i
n
t
)
;

// extra operations

};

The "type field" k is important to permit operations which include draw ( ) and rotate
Of shape they are managing (in a Pascal-like language, one would possibly use a variant recordwith tag k). The function draw ( ) is probably described like this:

V
o
i
d
s
h
a
p
e
:
:
d
r
a
w
(
)
{
S
w
i
t
c

```
h
(
k
)
{
c
a
s
e
c
i
r
c
l
e
:
/
/
d
r
a
w
a
c
i
r
c
l
e
B
r
```

e

a

k

;

c

a

s

e

t

r

i

a

n

g

l

e

:

/

/

d

r

a

w

a

t

r

i

a

n

g

l

e
b
r
e
a
k
;
C
a
s
e
s
q
u
a
r
e
:

```
// draw a square
}}
```

This is a large number. Capabilities along with draw ( ) have to "know about" all the sorts of shapes there are. Consequently, the code for this type of characteristic grows every time a brand-new shape is brought to the device. If you define a brand-new shape, every operationon a shape have to be tested and (probably) modified. You aren't able to upload a new shape to a device except you have got get entry to the supply code for every operation. Because adding a brand-new form entails "touching" the code of every essential operation on shapes,it requires awesome skill set and potentially introduces bugs into the code dealing with other (older) shapes. The choice of illustration of precise shapes can get significantly cramped through the requirement that (as a minimum a number of) their representation should suit into the normally constant sized framework presented through the definition of the overall kind shape.

The Simula inheritance mechanism presents a solution. First, specify a class that defines the general properties of all shapes:

C
l
a
s
s
s
h
a
p
e
{
p
o
i
n
t
c
e
n
t
e
r

```
;
C
o
l
o
r
c
o
l
;
// ... Public :
```

```
Point where() { return center; }
Void move(point to) { center =
to; draw(); ) virtual void draw();
Virtual void rotate (int) ;
// ...
};
```

The functions for which the calling interface may be described, however where the implementation cannot be described besides for a selected shape, had been marked "digital" (the Simula and C++ time period for "can be redefined later in a category derived from this one"). Given this definition, standard capabilities manipulating shapes were written:

```
Void rotate_all(shape** v, int size, int angle)
// rotate all members of vector "v"
of size "size" "angle" degrees (For
(int i = O; i < size; i++) v[i]
.rotate(angle);
)
```

To outline a particular shape, we have to say that it is a shape and specify its particular properties (which includes the virtual function):

C
l
a
s
s
c

i
r
c
l
e
:
p
u
b
l
i
c
s
h
a
p
e
(
l
n
t
r
a
d
i
u
s
;
p
u
b

l

i

c

:

Void draw ( ) { /* ... */ };

Void rotate(int) {} // yes, the null function};

In C++, c1 as circle is said to be derived from class shape, and class shape is said to be a baseof class circle. An alternative terminology calls circle and shape subclass and superclass, respectively.

The key implementation concept became that the set of virtual functions in a category definesan array of pointers to functions, in order that a name of a digital characteristic is virtually an oblique characteristic name thru that array. There is one array in step per class and one pointer to such an array in every object of a class that has virtual functions.

Designed software wouldn't want the extensibility and openness provided by using virtual functions, in order that right evaluation might show which non-virtual functions will be referred to as at once. Therefore, the argument went, virtual functions have been actually a shape of inefficiency. But virtual functions were added in the language anyway.

3.5 Overloading

Several human beings had requested for the capacity to overload operators. Reluctant pointsto not to add overloading in C++:

1. Overloading become reputed to be tough to enforce so that compilers would grow totremendous size.
2. Overloading was reputed to be tough to educate and hard to outline precisely in orderthat manuals and tutorials would develop to giant length.
3. Code written the use of operator overloading became reputed to be inherently inefficient.
4. Overloading changed into reputed to make code incomprehensible.

If all of these conjectures were false, then overloading might remedy some real problems forC++ users. There had been folks that would really like to have complex numbers, matrices, and APL-like vectors in C++. There were folks that would really like range-checked arrays, multi-dimensional arrays, and strings in C++. There have been at the least two separate programs for which people desired to overload logical operators which includes I(or), & (and),and ^ (distinctive or). The way I saw it, the listing turned into long and might grow with the scale and the variety of the C++ consumer populace. My answer to [4], "overloading makes code difficult to understand," become that several of the programmers, whose opinions werevalued and whose experience became measured in many years, claimed that their code would become cleaner in the event that they had overloading. So, what if you'll write difficult to understand code with overloading? It's miles possible to put in writing obscure code in any language. Its topics extra how a feature may be used properly than how it could be misused.First it was discovered that use of class with over-loaded operators, such as complex and string, changed into pretty easy and didn't placed a main burden at the programmer. Subsequent a guide released, the guide sections to prove that the delivered complexity wasn'ta serious problem; the forty-two-page manual needed less than a page and a half more. So, the first implementation in hours using most effective 18 strains of extra code in Cfront.

Certainly, these kinds of problems were not genuinely tackled in this strict sequential order. But, the focal point of the paintings did begin with application issues and slowly drifted to implementation troubles.

In retrospect, the complexity of the definition and implementation problems and compounded these troubles by seeking to isolate overloading mechanisms from the relaxation of the language semantics. The latter become done out of erroneous worry of perplexing customers.

Overload print ( ) ;

Should precede declarations of an overloaded

function print, which includesVoid print(int) ;

Void print (const char*) ;

Additionally, insisted that ambiguity manipulate should take place in two stages so that resolutions concerning built-in operators and conversions would constantly take precedence over resolutions related to person-defined operations. Maybe the latter changed into inevitable, given the priority for C compatibility and the chaotic nature of the C conversion regulations for built-in types. These conversions do now not constitute a lattice; for instance, implicit conversions are allowed each from into to drift and from waft to int. But, the policiesfor ambiguity resolution have been too complicated, triggered surprises, and needed to be revised for launch 2.0.

Requiring express overload declarations become undeniable wrong and the requirement become dropped in release 2.0.

3.6 References

References had been delivered basically to aid operator overloading. C passes each function argument by means of value, and in which passing an object by using value might beinefficient or beside the point the user can bypass a pointer. This strategy doesn't work whereoperator overloading is used. If so, notational comfort is vital so that a user can't anticipate to insert address of operators if the objects are massive.

Troubles with debugging ALGOL 68 convinced that having references that did not trade what object they stated after initialization, was an excellent component. Due to the fact C++ has each recommendations and references, it does not want operations for distinguishing operations at the reference itself from operations on the object cited (like Simula), or the sortof deductive mechanism hired by using ALGOL 68.

It's essential that const references can be initialized by way of non-lvalues and lvalues of types that require conversion. Specifically, that is what lets in a FORTRAN feature to be referred toas with a steady:

Extern "Fortran" go with the " float sqrt (const flow&); // °&' means reference sqrt(2); // callby way of reference

Jonathan Shopiro was deeply worried inside the discussions

that brought about the introduction of references. Similarly, to the obvious makes use of references, together with argument, taken into consideration the ability to apply references as return sorts critical. Thisallowed to have a very simple index operator for a string class:

```
Class String { // ...
Char& operator [] (int index); // subscript operator // return a reference
};
Void f(String& s)
{
Char cl = ...
S[i] = cl; //
assign to
operator [] 's
result // ...
Char c2 = s[i];
// assign
operator [] 's
result
}
```

The consideration permitting separate features for left-hand and right-hand side use of afeature but considered the use of references the easier opportunity, even though this implied to introduce extra "helper classes" to resolve a few issues where returning a simple referencewasn't sufficient.

3.7 Constants (const)

In operating systems, it's far common to have get access to a few pieces of memory controlled without delay or circuitously through bits: one which indicates whether or not a user can writeto it and one that shows whether a user can read it. This concept appeared without delay relevant to C++ and [taken into consideration allowing every kind to be distinctive read onlyor write only. The notion is focused on specifying interfaces instead of on offering symbolic constants for C. Clearly, a read-only value is a symbolic constant, but the scope of the conceptis far greater. To start with, it was proposed to read-only but now not read-only pointers. Sometime later, the ANSI C committee (X3J]!) Was formed and the const proposal resurfacedthere and have become a part of ANSI/[SO C.
But, within the interim [had experimented similarly with const in C with lessons anddiscovered that const become a beneficial opportunity to macros for representing constants best if an international consts were implicitly local to their compilation unit. Best if so, shouldthe compiler without problems deduce that their value truly did not alternate and allow simple consts in steady reviews and for that reason avoid allocating space for such constantsand use them in constant expressions. C did no longer undertake this rule. This makes constsfar less useful in C than in C++ and leaves C depending on the preprocessor in which C++ programmers can use nicely typed and scoped consts.

3.8 Memory Management

Long earlier the primary C with classes program was written, Bjarne Stroustrup knew that free store (dynamic memory) would be used extra closely in a language with classes than in traditional C programs. This turned into the reason for the introduction of the new and deleteoperators in C with Classes. The new operator that each allocates memory from the free storeand invokes a constructor to ensure initialization turned into borrowed from Simula. The delete operator was a necessary complement because Bjarne Stroustrup did not want C withlessons to rely on a garbage collector. The argument for the new operator may be summarizedlike this. Could you rather write:

```
X* p = new X(2);
Struct X * p =
(struct X *)
malloc(sizeof(struc
t X));If (p == O)
error("memory
exhausted");
P->init (2) ;
```

And in which version are you maximum likely to make a screw up? The arguments towards it,which had been voiced pretty much load at the time, have been "however we don't actually need it," and "but a person can have used new as an identifier." both observations are correct, of course.

Introducing "operator new" for this reason made the use of free save extra convenient and much less errors prone. This expanded its use even in addition so that the C free store allocation habitual m a l l o c ( ) used to enforce new became the most not unusual overall performance bottleneck in actual systems. This turned into no real wonder both; the only hassle become what to do approximately it. Having real packages spend 50 percentage or more in their time in malloc ( ) wasn't desirable.

Bjarne Stroustrup discovered consistent with-class allocators and deallocators very powerful. The fundamental idea is that free store memory usage is dominated by way of the allocation and deallocation of plenty of small gadgets from only a few instructions. Take over the allocation of those items in a separate allocator and you can shop both time and space for those objects and also lessen the quantity of fragmentation of the overall free store. The mechanism provided for 1.0, "assignments to this," changed into too low level and error prone and turned into changed with the aid of a cleaner solution in 2.0.

Observe that static and automatic (stack allotted) objects had been continually feasible and that the only memory control strategies relied closely on such objects. The string class became a standard example; here string objects are normally on the stack in order that they require no explicit memory management, and the free store they depend on is controlled completely and invisibly to the user with the aid of the String member functions.

3.9 Type Checking

The C++ kind checking rules were the result of experiments with the C with classes. All characteristic calls are checked at bring together time. The checking of trailing arguments can be suppressed through explicit specification in a feature statement. That is crucial to allow C'sprint f ():

```
Int printf(const char* ...) ;
// accept any argument after
// the initial character string
// ...
Printf("date: %s %d 19%d\n", month, day, year); / / maybe right
```

Numerous mechanisms have been supplied to relieve the withdrawal signs and symptoms that many C programmers feel when they first revel in strict checking. Overriding kind checking using the ellipsis changed into the most drastic and least advocated of these. Characteristic name overloading and default arguments [Stroustrup 1986b] made it possible to provide the arrival of a single function taking a selection of argument lists withoutcompromising type safety. The stream I/O system demonstrates that the weak checking wasn't essential even for I/O.

Conclusion

C++ is the language that is used anywhere however in particular in systems programming and embedded structures. Here system programming way for developing the running structures or drivers that interface with hardware. Embedded system method matters that are cars, robotics, and appliances. It is having a higher or wealthy network and developers, which helps in the smooth hiring of builders and on line solutions without difficulty. Uses of C++ is known as the safest language due to its security and functions. It is the primary language for any developer to start, who is inquisitive about operating in programming languages. It is straightforward to analyze, as it's far natural idea-based language. Its syntax is quite simple, which makes it clean to write down or develop and mistakes may be effortlessly replicated. Before the use of any other language, programmers preferred to analyze C++ first and then they used different languages. However maximum of the developers try to stay with C++ handiest due to its huge sort of usage and compatibility with more than one structures and software.

CPSIA information can be obtained
at www.ICGtesting.com
Printed in the USA
BVHW042140280521
608097BV00009B/387

9 781802 263220